THE ESSENTIALS OF STYLE

Spring Journal Books
Studies in Archetypal Psychology Series

Series Editor
Greg Mogenson

Other titles in the Series

Dialectics & Analytical Psychology:
The El Capitan Canyon Seminar
Wolfgang Giegerich, David L. Miller, Greg Mogenson

Collected English Papers
Vol I: The Neurosis of Psychology: Primary Papers
towards a Critical Psychology
Vol. II: Technology and the Soul
Wolfgang Giegerich

Raids on the Unthinkable:
Freudian *and* Jungian Psychoanalyses
Paul Kugler

Northern Gnosis: Thor, Baldr, and the Volsungs
in the Thought of Jung and Freud
Greg Mogenson

The Wounded Researcher: A Depth Psychological
Approach to Research
Robert Romanyshyn

The Sunken Quest, the Wasted Fisher, the Pregnant Fish:
Postmodern Reflections on Depth Psychology
Ronald Schenk

Fire in the Stone: The Alchemy of Desire
Stanton Marlan, ed.

THE ESSENTIALS OF STYLE

A Handbook for Seeing and Being Seen

Benjamin Sells

Spring Journal Books
New Orleans, Louisiana

Published by
Spring Journal, Inc.;
627 Ursulines Street #7
New Orleans, Louisiana 70116
Tel.: (504) 524-5117
Fax: (504) 558-0088
Website: www.springjournalandbooks.com

Cover art:
Margot McLean, *Pyriform Recess*, 1990
mixed media on linen, 48" x 60"

Cover design by
Michael Mendis
24 Blackfriars Street
London, Ont. N6H 1K6
Canada

Printed in Canada
Text printed on acid-free paper

Library of Congress Cataloging-in-Publication Data Pending

Contents

First Impressions

It is remarkable that each thing of the world appears as it does and is distinguishable from all other things. Even the mass produced objects of the assembly line, designed and built to meet the specifications of sameness, can be distinguished by those who know how to look. Variety, it seems, is the way of the world.

Over the years there have been many debates about what distinguishes one thing from another. Philosophers have argued that the qualities that make a thing unique belong to the thing itself or, to the contrary, that such distinguishing qualities lie in the eye and mind of the beholder. Psychologists have mostly ignored the psychology of things in general to argue instead over what constitutes the unique in people—arguments that keep with a larger cultural view denying "psyche" or "soul" to non-human entities. With regard to people, psychology has favored ideas such as identity and self, seeking to discover through introspection and historical reconstruction the secret core that makes a person what he or she "truly" is. Such ideas markedly assume that what others see in a person is false and misleading, while the "true self" remains available only to the private eye.

In the world of style, however, such arguments miss the point insofar as they lay claim to answers and explanations that belong to an abstract world once removed from the things they claim to deduce and define. Style would set aside questions about the veracity of such claims to see them instead as stylized displays in their own right. Taken in themselves, such claims are merely further examples of the many ways in which the world presents itself. They are displays that can be appreciated without need of agreement or allegiance. The world of style, then, is not revealed through abstract debates or by turning our eyes and hearts away from the things of the world in an introspective quest for self-discovery. Rather the world of style is a world of display and perception, which for style are two words describing the same event.

Style avoids arguments drawn from other perspectives that would block and limit its basic interest in things. Distinctions such as manifest or latent, inner or outer, self or other do little to aid style, which prefers to imagine that what we call latent or inner actually points to limitations in appreciation rather than to metaphysical realms of the lost, private, or repressed. For style, the things of the world are always right there, looking back at us and our looking. From this perspective there can be no trees falling alone in the woods because trees are never alone and there can be no secret selves defined apart from the other things of the world. For style, such purported paradoxes belong only to the gaming mind at play.

In the world of style all things appear as presences before the other things of the world. Nothing exists in isolation. When guided by style, aesthetic concerns of precision and appreciation trump the more abstract ends of answers and explanations. It is enough for style to concentrate on being in the world in the most beautiful and appropriate manner possible, where beauty refers not to the pretty or cute but to the presence of things appearing as they are. Socrates, for example, was said to be beautiful not because of a handsome visage but because he was as he appeared to be. He was at home in his style.

An old proverb grasps style as it is intended in this book: *stylus virum arguit*—style proclaims the person. According to this view it is not we who choose among various styles according to whim or personal preference, but style that constitutes us and makes possible our choosing. *We already are before we decide to be,* and this immediate presence, borne by the other things of the world, is the work of style. Style sets us before many eyes, showing us for what we are and what we can be quite apart from our thoughts about ourselves and the desires we create. Style proclaims a thing's unique presence, and through its many proclamations style creates a welcoming world in which each thing has a place.

If this way of imagining style sounds odd or ephemeral, this is due in part to what we have done to the idea of style. Nowadays, style often is associated with transient and superficial fashion. Bell-bottoms come and go, in and out of style. Long hair this season, shaved and sculpted the next. Style has even come to imply a kind of fakeness, as if a person's style is a façade or mask showing a false face to the world while hiding another, presumably "truer" face that is shown only in private.

The problem here is confusing the kind of style that proclaims things as they are with affectations designed to pass for style. The former relies on direct appreciation and is dependent upon a supportive world; the latter emanates from self-conscious choices and the currently accepted vogue. And so we have come to say that the runway model is stylish in her *haute couture*, wearing as she does the latest in fashion from celebrated designers. Or we associate style with flourish and excess, pointing to the gaudy celebrity dressed in his funny clothes and loud manners. Here style is reduced to mannequins draped in the fashions of others or is left overexposed in glossy pictures on slick paper. We have even come to think that such affectations help to establish our individuality by setting us apart from the crowd. And so we seek to mimic such efforts, wearing clothes and habits that project the style we want to have and show the face we want to show. If only we have the right car, the right clothes, and the right look, we think, we can really *be* somebody.

But there is a distinction between style that seeks to adopt the looks and mannerisms of others and style that exists in the midst of such a quest and makes such a quest possible. For the style that proclaims us, there is no possibility of a quick change or makeover that will produce us anew. Rather, each thing is already and always distinguished from the other things of the world, and there is no need for affectation to accomplish this distinction. The style that proclaims us renders each thing visible to the other things of the world, making each thing appear as it does even if this appearance is not apparent or available to the thing's own reflective experience. Style reverses the old Cartesian dictum of "I think, therefore I am," to proclaim "I am, therefore I think"—first presence then reflection. The mirror and its frame, mainstays for the kind of style that depends on reflection and affectation, is of little use to the style that places us immediately before other things. A mirror gives only a flat reflection, not an embodied presence existing in a multi-dimensional world of perspective, composition, and depth. Style reminds us that no thing can see its own fullness and that our backsides are as much a mystery to us as the dark side of the moon.

What matters most, then, is not what we choose to take from the styles of others, not the habits and affectations we try on, but how we go about doing all of these things. It is a mystery of style that you can dress two people in the same clothes and one will appear dull while the other is cut with flash. In the world of style each is recognized and honored as a proclamation of style. This is a delicate point—the act of our choosing, the roads we take and the roads we leave untraveled, are given by the style that already and always proclaims us. That I choose to look dapper and slick does in fact say much about me to the other things of the world. But whether I do, in fact, look dapper and slick is dependent on how the other things of the world perceive me, not on my personal view taken from my morning reflections. The other things of the world will see before I the incongruities of fashion and character, the mismatching of gilding and gait. Style proclaims us despite our efforts to be otherwise. We cannot long hide from eyes that see.

Attempts to purchase style ready-made off the rack or pulled from the minds of others are doomed endeavors. Trying to piece together a style from the styles of others turns us into symbols, representations instead of presentations. The loss here often is obscured by the illusion that our stylistic representations are actually helping us to become what we are seeking to become. This illusion is fostered by the apparent recognition we feel from others when they admire our symbolic handiwork. But what really has happened is that our symbols are being recognized by those already versed in such symbols. And so we come to depend on the right luggage or the newest running shoes to portray us in a certain light. If everyone in the circle I wish to join wears black then I, too, will wear black so that they, and I, will know that I belong to the circle. Wrapping ourselves in symbols can give us a sense of belonging and security, but symbols are notoriously fragile and fickle things.

Such symbolic efforts are pretenders to style, they attempt style by proxy. They are transient substitutes for the style that proclaims each thing as it is. What such attempts miss is that it is not the brand name on the hat that bestows style but the manner in which the hat is worn. One person can have the latest in everything and be a walking anachronism while another finds an old beret at the thrift store and looks like a movie star in disguise. The style that proclaims us cannot be reduced to slogan and symbol, and it cannot be chosen or discarded according to whim. Style becomes a parody when it becomes representation instead of presentation; left to its own devices, style gives us the world unfettered.

Nothing a person does is ever out of style. Style cannot be avoided. That I spend hours going through the fashion magazines trying to find a look that's right for me is itself an indication of style; maybe even more so than the resulting purchases I make or the clothes I might wear trying to match the models. The question is how to see what style shows to us with a depth and breadth of imagination that takes everything in without resorting to definitions and restrictive categories. That a serial killer seemed like such a nice, quiet young man to his neighbors is not an aberration, but a further detail that must be accounted for in our imagination of the killer's style. And my conviction that despite my job as an accountant I am really a poet is a telling indication of style referring not to what I "really am" but to a way of being in the world that is held by such convictions and thinks in such terms. From this perspective, each thing is as it is and cannot be otherwise. It is style, not we, that proclaims how things are.

Perhaps the greatest gift of style is that it is mostly perceived and appreciated by others. These perceptions and appreciations are not passive affairs, but rather help to constitute the style of things. Style claims that there is no thing that is not beholden to other things for its very essence. Nothing can contribute to the world without that world at the same time making such contributions possible. Nothing and no one is self-made, and to think otherwise assumes a cosmos submissive to the solitary individual. Indeed trying to define an individual in isolation from others is, from the perspective of style, a catastrophic mistake. And to think that I can appreciate my own style without the input of others who are largely responsible to and for my style ignores the constituting role of those things in my style. Style's simple message is that the things of the world see and appreciate at least as much if not more about my style than I can ever see or appreciate. Style proclaims that I am not a secret self locked away from prying, competitive eyes but a public presence made possible by a world that looks back and in so looking helps to shape my style.

This last idea is critical; without you there is no me. The things of the world are dependent upon one another, not because we form some kind of metaphysical unity, but because we are all here. Not because some beneficent transcendent force holds us together but because it is the nature of things to be interested and involved with one another. Things require one another's presence, and this simple fact does not need grand theories to justify it. Style encourages the things of the world to be what they can be, stimulating invention and opportunity and making the world a becoming place. In this world there can be no pianists without pianos, and no pianos without pianists. In this world when butterflies cannot reproduce because of feeding on genetically altered plants, all things taste extinction. And in this world the fact that whales can distinguish the songs of their fellows is not taken in the first instance as survival adaptability. Style wonders instead what could be more natural than singing creatures appreciating song. And it also wonders why our interpretation must turn the whale's appreciation into an ugly act of self-interest. Does this not say more about us and our interpretations than about the whale?

In the world of style, the greater part of my style lies beyond my skin and bones and in the fashioning hands of other things. Introspection, then, shutters our eyes to where style mostly appears by turning us inward and away from the other things of the world. In the world of style, beauty of presence, interest in the greater world, the crafting of appropriate responses, and the welcoming arms of affinity form the royal road to style.

Style is content to remain within an aesthetic world. Faced with a mystery such as why some affinities seem to last a lifetime while others come and go with the wind, style avoids the distractions of explanation and keeps its focus on the affinities that are present. It is more important for style to do right by the affinities that grace our lives whenever and however they appear than to make determinations about why some things stay and some go. This does not mean that style does not welcome and entertain the ideas and interpretations desired and spun by the intellect, but only that such things are considered first and always as displays of style. For style, there is an aesthetic basis to all experience of whatever sort, including our explanations of things.

There is nothing more intimate than one's style. But this intimacy relies on an imagining world that provides a public place for style to do its work. That so many people become nervous or afraid when appearing before a group of other people has less to do with issues of self-esteem or potential embarrassment than on the more basic fact that we really do exist within the imaginations of all those watchful eyes. What we feel in such moments is our dependence on the other things of the world. We want to look good and to make a good impression, and we want this not from vanity or pride alone but because how we look and the impressions we make are living testimony to our presence among the other things of the world. Only a fool doesn't care what other people think. The thoughts of others are part of their imagination about us, and without such imagination we cannot appear, we cannot be. This doesn't mean we slavishly live our lives according to the wishes and demands of others; it means only that the things of the world know as much about us as we know about ourselves.

We do not have to search for style because style is always already here, already proclaiming us. Style is not hidden but apparent— it is all in the looking. If we want to learn about style, then, the place to look is to the things of the world that style proclaims. How to look, and the inherent double meaning of that phrasing, is a central theme of this book.

Over and over again people lose themselves in introspective quests. I am a poet, says the accountant, when the facts of his life suggest that again and again people have turned to him for his gifts with numbers and balance. Still, like a poet, he, too, keeps and makes accounts, but this stylistic kinship is lost to a mind trained to believe in the lost.

What are we to do? Are we to ignore what the world reveals to us because it does not match what we want to believe about ourselves? For style, what matters is that the tension between the accountant's self-conscious image and what others see in the accountant is itself an attribute of his presence that is revealed by style. After all, he could not be the accountant he is without his imaginings about really being a poet and the poet of his imagination could live nowhere else but with this man—neither, really, are unrequited though it be part of their style to feel otherwise. For style, there is no need to denigrate the accountant so as to free the imprisoned poet. What is needed is a broader imagination in which both accountant and poet are seen in the context of style. Whether the accountant and the poet can exist separately is of no concern to style. What matters is that they are presented together and so they are taken together. Style does not interpret or analyze. Style appreciates.

Style teaches us that it is a great mistake to ignore the facts of life. We cannot avoid what the things of the world call upon us to do simply because they don't fit our own views of ourselves. To do otherwise leaves us broken and misplaced. There is so little virtue in following only one's own wishes. Contrary to the aims and claims of self-improvement that belie us with inflated thoughts about ourselves, it is better to remember that the thoughts and images we have about ourselves are no more trustworthy or insightful than the thoughts and images that the other things of the world have about us. Cast your own mind over your memory. Think of the many times in your life when you have been sure about some attribute or desire only to discover later how mistaken you were. With such memories, and they are abundant in us all, why do we persist in believing what we tell ourselves about ourselves? What does it take to make us realize that we are not solitary individuals and that our private views about ourselves are merely other voices to be heard? The things of the world know what we can do and where we are needed as well if not better than we do, and often provide more clarity than we can muster ourselves. To further our interest in style, then, we must reawaken our hearing to voices other than our own.

––––––––

The ancient antecedents of the word "style" refer to a pointed tool used for writing—hence our "stylus." According to scholars, the spelling of style with the letter "y" is likely an error based on the assumption that the word derived from the Greek word for column or pillar. Mistake or not, the word style brings together the images of a written world where each thing is inscribed with intention and specificity, and a world in which each thing stands alongside others as part of a larger plan of mutual support and adornment.

To imagine style in terms of an instrument for writing also suggests that we are inscribed by the styles of others as we inscribe our styles on them. Nothing passes without a trace. In the world of style all things contribute to a written world, offering their hands in its on-going creation and maintenance. And, because writing and reading go together, style teaches that we learn to make our mark at the same time that we learn to read the inscriptions of our fellows. To leave a proper impression, then, style says that we must learn to regard the handiwork of others with as much intensity and consideration as we do our own.

We learn to read style by learning to read the world. We learn to read the world by learning to read style. Not chicken or egg but chicken and egg. The key is maintaining a perspective that sees the things of the world as presentations in their own right, gifts of style that add their indispensable part to the on-going pageantry of life. For style, everything is aesthetic, everything a display. The painting in the gallery is there first of all to be appreciated, not analyzed or reduced to this or that school of painting or to the artist's biography. It is a presence deserving of our interest that offers enormous potential to those who are drawn to it. Some will pass it by with scarcely a look. But others will travel great distances just to be in the same room.

The important thing for style is to allow the painting to present itself in its own fashion. This means that we, would-be readers of style, must watch and wait, letting the painting reveal itself to us in its own way and in its own time. If we come armed with prejudgments we will not see the painting but a reproduction filtered through a haze of expectations. In the world of style it is better to appreciate than to assume, and so style encourages us to be patient and respectful of things as they choose either to reveal themselves or not.

Letting things show us what they are without preconception on our part is very difficult. And it becomes more so if we allow ourselves to traffic in symbols and code words. Such symbols and code words suck the life out of things. They attempt to corral the many things of the world so as to tame them to this or that ideology. Symbolic constructions such as gender, race, and ethnicity, for example, can curtail appreciation and limit style's insatiable interest in the particularity of things. Similarly, the code words and weighted rhetoric of fundamentalism obscure the many things of the world with a settling fog. A hundred people can call themselves Democrats or pro-life or feminists or white and none of them will mean, can mean, the same thing. For style, each proclamation is a field of richness and diversity. Nothing is only an example of something else.

One function of style is to draw attention to the actual qualities of a thing so we might better appreciate it for what it is. Only by letting a thing articulate itself can we begin to appreciate it. Otherwise we simply toss the thing into a labeled drawer and forget about it. And once labeled a thing loses both interest and life. That a person claims to be a Democrat tells us nothing about his or her style until we come to see what manner of Democrat he or she is. How does this claimed allegiance interact with the other aspects of the person's life? What ideas are tied to this word for this person? How do they live this word in their daily actions? Only in the greater context of the other things of the world can we begin to appreciate this proffered detail, much the same way we come to know a fictional character through the slow accretion of details and mannerisms that educate our imaginations about them and lead us into their styles.

Indeed for style all things appear as fictional entities. This does not mean they are not real, whatever that means, but only that style takes them in and through their imaginative dimensions. They remain images. Just as we come to know a character through following the author's depiction, so we might imagine our fellow things of the world in a similar light. What to make of that peculiar habit our friend has? If we were to read about a character like our friend who had such a habit, what would we make of it? Not by way of explanation or understanding, but as a further proclamation of our friend by his or her style. What does this habit, with its nuances and tics, contribute to our friend's style? We know the habit is somehow necessary, else it would not be part of our friend's presence, and so we watch and wait and let this habit show us more of our friend. If we try to analyze the habit we quickly leave our friend behind as we go off in search of causes and effects. But in the world of style things are not the result of cause and effect; they simply are there to be appreciated.

Style is not only what we perceive but also how we perceive; to see style we must look with style. When I look into a mirror and recognize a continuing image looking back at me, perhaps it is not some enduring "I" that I see but rather the style of my looking that has remained over time. In other words, perhaps what I perceive as enduring lies not in how I look in the sense of what I have on, etc., which obviously changes, but how I look, i.e. the nature of how I perceive. According to style the how of my looking influences how I look.

The aesthetic tradition suggests that we engage our own styles by learning to appreciate the styles of others, which means that we must learn to discern with an aesthetic eye attuned to style. If there is an aesthetic basis to all experience then our individual styles give us the ability to perceive in certain ways. By educating this ability, and respecting the things it shows to us, we also educate our individual styles. In fact, the more we learn to perceive with style the less compelled we seem to be in fixating on our own. Style opens us beyond ourselves to a stylish world, easing the anxieties of introspection and the isolation they engender.

It helps to remember that most mysteries remain mysteries. All knowing has its limits. So style keeps mystery constantly in mind, aware of the paradox that style is both visible and invisible at once. Through this paradox we learn about the spectrum of the visible, how a thing both sees and is seen, and how even as style proclaims the person, it cannot be encompassed by the person only. Let us remember that there is something wondrous about how one child reaches out right away while another pulls back. How old the young can seem, the small hand making an already old gesture. Are these vestiges of style incarnate? A mystery.

The perpetual desire to be "in style" suggests that style is always up to date and then some, forever outdistancing us with its enduring presence. Things might fall in and out of style, but style is always in fashion. Perhaps this means that style does not belong to time at all but rather to that which is out-of-time altogether, neither past, present, nor future. Or perhaps style encompasses time, giving particularity to endurance. Style seems to appear without reference to our meager ways of imagining time, showing up in memories of the past, anticipations of the future, and in the fabric of everyday life. Perhaps style is connected somehow to the eternal, just as the mystery of style indelibly links our peculiarities to those of other peculiar beings, both living and dead, mortal and immortal, in whose styles we share. But to associate style with the eternal does not divorce style from the routines of everyday practice. Style is found nowhere more surely than in the facts of daily life. Even inspiration appears in context, like an old song coming from the jukebox in the corner.

Style, then, is the mysterious something that makes things appear as they do and not otherwise. In this sense, style is the display of eachness — each thing appearing as it does in the context of other things. A thing's style presents it as both unique and common. In fact, for style the unique and the common cannot be separated. What is uniqueness, after all, but the inevitable configurations of the commonplace? Style therefore distinguishes each thing from the other things of the world without removing it from its particular time, place, and circumstance. And, when the things of the world act, these actions, too, appear precisely configured, as if guided by some invisible logic in keeping with style's proclamations.

———

As we live, style finds us various avenues of expression, directing us to particular endeavors and wrapping our hands around particular tools. We gravitate to certain areas that although apparently disparate are held together by our styles. Watch a person doing dishes and that same person directing a million dollar project and you will see something familiar in how they do both acts. Not something the same, no, which would be identity's over-reaching conclusion, but something familiar, as if one act is related to the other through the person's style, each person his or her own next of kin. Our every act then presents a microcosm of style with each act related to all of the other acts that contribute to and reflect our style. Style therefore requires that we take appropriate action in accord with the imaginal demands of our lives. We cannot avoid, and so do better to embrace, the requirements of style. *Stylus virum arguit*—style proclaims, not requests, and so we must adhere to its proclamations.

Style belongs neither to hyped rhetoric of exclusive alternatives and adversarial debates nor to bland claims of wholeness, unity, and oneness. Such rhetoric fronts for metaphysical claims that would divide the world to appease ideological ends, while style can only look at such claims and the worlds they produce, perceiving and appreciating them for what they are in terms of the styles they display. Style allows us to see that there is no "inside" that is private only to me and no "outside" that exists beyond such an insular privacy. Style resists such ideas because style is not an ideological stance but a practice of imagination, an aesthetic discipline.

Style limits its consideration to imagination and aesthetics because that is where style belongs. Style is in no position to proclaim philosophical ideas right or wrong, good or bad. Instead, style remains dedicated to careful and appreciative perceiving. Style stays put, urging us to take more care in our awareness of things and in how we present ourselves in a vibrant and inherently beautiful world. Style remains true to its limitations and thereby to itself, offering its many perspectives to the other things of the world as pleasantries to abide and enjoy.

When guided by style we are no longer bound by theoretical restrictions but follow matters of propriety learned through intimate interaction with the other things of the world. Once we set aside symbolic attempts to be this or that according to some preconceived plan our styles become free to take their, and our, heads. As we will see in the pages to come, through style we find the tools, teachers, and traditions that suit us best. Temperament, taste, and talent appear and press us into service on style's behalf, guiding us through the aesthetic possibilities given by the other things of the world. Obstacles to style are met and overcome, and, through proper care and obedience to the possibilities that style provides, style proclaims us.

PART I

The World of This Book

PRESENCE

INTEREST

RESPONSE

AFFINITY

CHAPTER ONE

Presence

There are many ways to imagine the world, each with its own potentials and pitfalls, advantages and disadvantages. Because our interest is style, we begin by imagining the world in a manner befitting that interest. To read the many styles of the world, we must first imagine a world in which style is not an incidental concern but a main one, a continuing focus. For the world of this book, style matters most.

We will begin our work by considering four ideas—presence, interest, response, and affinity. Together these ideas provide a way of imagining the world that emphasizes style throughout. That there are many other ways of imagining the world is assumed. Indeed we will see that each style co-exists with its own cosmos, the things of the world made possible by style as style is made possible by the things of the world. From the perspective of style, then, the things of the world appear as images in the context of imagination. Style assumes a cosmology of imagination that in turn necessarily involves the imagination of many cosmologies.

The world of style is a vibrant place in which each thing of the world presents itself to the other things of the world. For style, each thing both is a presence and has presence; that is, it is present before others, it brings with it a sense of proximity and place, is noteworthy and compelling, has bearing, includes invisible powers, and impresses itself on the other things of the world, altering and influencing those things. Presence includes all of these aspects at once.

From the perspective of style, to be present is to be present before others. Without the things of the world to spark our interest, and to be interested in us, style does not appear. Looking at and being looked back at is what it means to be present in the world of style. But keep in mind that for style all things are capable of doing the looking, and all things are capable of presence, interest, response, and affinity. Think how welcoming our own bed feels after a long trip, how secure a favorite kitchen knife feels in our hand, how surely a desert mesa holds its place, and how forlornly blue a hill becomes when scalped of its green. The things of the world are alive with eyes; they watch and their watching gives rise to the world. In this world it is never quite certain what is the stage and who are the players as all things can be present as actors, stagehands, backdrops, scenery, curtains, and audience at once.

A thing's presence before others can take many forms. When we think of a person's presence, for example, we can mean his or her physical presence or his or her presence in our lives as a significant and enduring image. Or we can mean the person's presence as it appears in our imagination when it comes to us, sometimes unbidden, to offer perspectives and advice, the way a teacher's voice reaches the student long after class is over. Or we can mean their adorned presence in our memories, laced with joy and grief. A person's presence can be in each and all of such instances, and persists as that peculiar something that strikes our imagination in a way unlike any other. And, at the same time, it is our peculiar imaginings about the person that nourish and encourage their presence, keeping it vital and alive.

To be present before others one must show oneself, and this showing is accomplished through style. Style presents a thing's presence as an overall impression, an impression that can neither be reduced to any single content nor inflated to transcendental form. We experience a thing's presence all at once, so to speak, as if all of its many characteristics had come together for a slightly out-of-focus group portrait. Presence shows us everything at once even though there is no way we can take it in all at once. Like gazing at the Grand Canyon, it's all there for the looking but who can fathom so much at once? Although style shows each thing with great particularity and is discernible with great precision there is nonetheless an ineffable air about a thing's presence. We don't seem capable of telling everything that we sense and feel about a thing's presence, much like a dream we have lived intimately but can never quite do justice in the telling.

When we feel a thing's presence, we feel its closeness. The lurking night or an almost inaudible whisper in the mind—in the presence of each of these things we feel something close, pressing. Presence is how proximity feels, and so presence stands as a ward to isolation or singularity. Presence lets us know that nothing stands alone and that the many things of the world always appear in the context of the rest of things, with each thing being just where and as it is according to the needs of style.

Style allows us to distinguish among the many presences that hold us close, even reaching into what we imagine to be our most intimate recesses, finding us there to press their case. The things of the world, registered by imagination through their presence, are irrepressible; they cannot be silenced or shut out. Even after death, say many spiritual traditions, we are accompanied by them. The proximity we feel through presence is the feeling of being in the world, and it is the ability of many things to hold one another close that makes the world possible. And it is style that makes this closely-held world discernible, appreciable, and communicable.

Although close, the other things of the world retain their own places, thereby reminding us that place is a necessary aspect of all things. Where a thing is helps to determine what and how it is. Places are presences in their own right, and so we can imagine that particular places favor some activities over others. A ritual dance born of the jungle is lost and a little pathetic if done in a shopping mall for the amusement of bored consumers. Places make room for things to happen that could not happen elsewhere, and indeed without place there is no place for anything to occur. Location, location, location.

Presences interact with one another like shapes straining to fit. One of life's opportunities is encountering the presence of others, rubbing shoulders and touching borders with the other things of the world. Sometimes we share common borders of great length with a particular thing (we have a lot in common), and sometimes we do not (we really could not find anything to talk about, I can't get into this tune, etc.). Shared borders can elicit strong feelings among things (feelings that are not necessarily benign or welcoming), while other things that share no direct borders are nonetheless relevant and important for one another. We can learn much about things by observing the borders they share and watching how they treat their neighbors, both near and far.

Another attribute of presence is bearing—to have presence is to have bearing. From the perspective of style, bearing has many meanings that each bear on how things appear. Bearing can mean being distinguished, both in the sense of something being discernible in its own right and in having an air of integrity and dignity. Bearing can suggest direction and purpose, even when direction and purpose cannot be known with any certainty—confidence being more reliable than certitude. Bearing can refer to the fullness and fruitfulness of life, as when a fruit tree is ready for bearing. And it can designate strength and support, as in a load-bearing wall. These multiple meanings of integrity, purpose, fecundity, and strength all help to distinguish and qualify a thing's presence to the imaginations of others.

Ghosts and other spirits often present themselves only in terms of their felt presence. They appear as vestiges of their old selves, discernible as being present while at the same moment displaying their absence through their very appearance. Indeed part of their power and influence comes from their being present while they also are not here. In the world of this book, all things are imagined as coming complete with ghosts, spirits, and associated invisible presences of unimaginable diversity and complexity that contribute to a thing being what it is and not something else. The unseen and unknowable, which is most of things, are essential to the display of style and the presence of things. And so what we might call a hunch we might also imagine as an anonymous tip coming from unseen quarters, what we call having a dream we might imagine as receiving a guest, and what we call writing a story we might imagine as taking dictation. Given its penchant for imaginative language, style need not set aside the actual experiences of life for fear of breaching an argument over literalities. Untold numbers of writers have reported the feeling of taking dictation while writing, but none need posit a supernatural world to support the feeling.

It is the nature of invisible presences to work invisibly, and they often are capable of the greatest influence precisely where and when we are most sure they are absent. Often the presence of a thing is revealed most clearly, if indirectly, through the influence it has on the appearance and activities of others. So when we are considering making a decision, for example, or are thinking something through, activities that we think are rational and objective, we in fact are in the midst of presences having their own viewpoints and desires. Our decisions and explanations always appease some invisible group of special interest.

From the perspective of style, then, much about a thing can be determined by the company it keeps, and these accompanying presences can be expected to influence all aspects of the thing, visible or otherwise. Style reminds us that invisible things display themselves through their influence as revealed in the presence and style of other things. Who can speak of freedom or love, for example, without referring to things that animate and give presence to such ideals?

As we will see throughout this book, reading style requires being able to observe how things act around one another. The presence of a thing often becomes clearer when we see how its appearance alters the context in which it appears. The lion might give us an immediate feeling of power and danger, but watch the gazelles leap away and the birds take to air and we know a little more about the lion. For style, a thing's presence includes the responses to it by the other things of the world. We will discuss this critical idea more fully in Chapter Three, but response also belongs here, with presence. Although the abstracting mind can split the responses to a thing from the appearance of the thing, in the world style the two ideas belong inextricably together.

Style is forever arranging and re-ordering the many things of the world. For style the world is an aesthetic field offering ongoing opportunities for appearance and appreciation. It makes no sense from the perspective of style to talk about a world apart from the things of the world. For style, "world" refers simply to the infinite arrangements made possible by things. Just as many traditions say it was the other animals who taught humans how to live and imagine, style says it is the many things of the world that make possible our imaginings about the world.

An ancestral voice, a city alley, a rock in a garden, your next door neighbor—each are differentiated and made perceptible by their particular styles. Each thing of the world therefore offers opportunities to learn more about style. Everything is different, yes, but this difference holds everything in common—there is nothing that is not different from everything else. The eachness of things thereby proclaims our commonality. By showing us this world in all of its particularity, style makes everything feel at home. Style leaves nothing out, displaying in its own way the visible, the invisible, and everything in between.

As we become more attuned to style we see that what appears to be a single thing can be many things at once, sometimes even blending with other things. Your neighbor might sometimes speak with an ancestral voice, the city alley might contain more than shadows and smells, and the rock in the garden might be more a neighbor to you than the person next door. Style imagines that each thing comprises many things. Although things can be distinguished and differentiated from one another with great specificity by their styles, the things of the world are nonetheless multiple by their very nature. Each thing is a multiplicity of potentials. Look at the youngest face and you will see more than one thing looking back. Even time coalesces in style, the adult already there in the child.

The presence of each thing is multiple both in its presentation and its potential, each thing a configuration of many styles and influences. This multiplicity is woven by style and presented as a cohesive thing through a thing's presence. From the perspective of style, it is important not to confuse the cohesion of a thing's presence with ideas claiming it to be a single thing, or to have this or that identity. Reducing anything to a single, stand-alone entity is a mistake of the mind, telling us more about the inability of certain styles of mind to entertain multiple perspectives than it does about the nature of things. Oneness is in the eye of the beholder, whereas from the perspective of style each thing is imagined as full of surprises and potentials.

The inherent multiplicity of things allows for many avenues to exist between the things of the world. And so to some degree what we learn about the style of one thing enriches our appreciation of the styles of others. As the many things of the world articulate themselves through their styles we begin to discover similarities and likenesses among them, perhaps seeing one thing in terms of another thing or even seeing one thing as within another. These opportunities for precise imaginings among and in between things evoke an intimacy that further awakens our interest in the things of the world. A good poem can show this at work by bringing together seemingly unrelated things in a carefully crafted context so as to reveal previously unseen connections. The poem not only shows the intimate connections of seemingly unrelated things but also gives birth to a new thing—the poetic image—to be appreciated in its own right.

Given the inherent multiplicity of things, nothing exists in a vacuum. All things bring with them many contexts born of their own multiplicity. Even the most common thing, such as a rock or a cup, cannot be what it is without the multiplicity of presences that constitute it as what it is. What you see might be what you get, but it is not all that you get. And so when we consider the context of a thing we must cast our imagination wide enough to make room not only for the multiplicity of contexts provided by the other things of the world but also for the multiplicity of contexts given by the thing itself. Each thing is a community, we might imagine, and this community will speak with differing voices at differing times and places. The task for those who would read the styles of things is to learn to hear and differentiate these voices.

The invisible contexts of a thing become more apparent to the imagination as we come closer to the particular presence and style of the thing. We can say a spear is a symbol for war, for example, and read about spears and war, and in so doing we will learn a little about the meaning of spears and war. But take the spear in hand, heft its weight and find its balance, let your thumb run the blade's taper to its sticking point and you will feel the palpable ambition of its invisible, and constituting, power. This feeling, this precise feeling, is impossible without the spear, and the spear is impossible without the feeling. There are no substitutes for the things of the world.

That the things of the world appear as they do is a mystery beyond final answer. It also is a great delight, and from the perspective of style we can imagine that the things of the world appear as they do because that is what they are here for, each thing existing as it does for the sheer pleasure of existing as it does. In this world each thing is a presence in its own right and joins with all other things to contribute to the beauty of things. This is a world in which style matters most.

CHAPTER TWO

Interest

Things appear and you are drawn to them. This ability to have one's attention drawn to something is a gift of imagination. You see a flash of red out of the corner of your eye and you turn to look. This turning is a show of interest. If the things of the world were not interesting then the flash would not divert our gaze. From the perspective of style, there is no sight without the appearance of things to excite our vision, no taste without tasty things, no smell without the world's bouquets, no touch without textures to caress, no hearing without the music of sound. And no love without that first desire to look.

The things of the world are home to our interests, beckoning us to their particular places and holding out attention by their particular styles. Two people walk hand-in-hand down the same shady lane and come home to tell different stories of what they saw: one comments on the newly painted house on the corner; the other didn't see the house but at some time during the walk finally did see the point of that movie they watched together last evening. From the perspective of style both of these viewings occur in the context of the walk — neither could happen otherwise. That two people look at the same scene and see different things is primarily a function of the inherent multiplicity of things and how they choose to show different aspects of themselves to different viewers. Just as each thing's style allows it to display itself to others, each thing's style also enables it to be called especially by particular things and to have its interest held there. Style is the world making itself interesting.

One of life's many pleasures is noticing. Our attentions are constantly called forth by the things of the world. In the world of style this enlivening of interest is attributed to the fact that the things of the world are interesting. Right from the start they present themselves as noteworthy. Look at me, says the old tree alone on the hill, its silhouette etched against the sky as if done for effect. Hear me, hums the tune to the singer. Ponder me, riddles the idea to the thinker. There is something compelling about the things of the world. Once in their presence we seem unable to be disinterested. And if one thing doesn't get our attention then another one will. The coins at the coin show reach out only to certain collectors, we might imagine, collectors with whom they share mutual interests and similar tastes and so will pass time well together. To someone else the coins are but old silver, and so to that person the coins remain reticent, turning a tarnished face and pretending only to be loose change. In the world of style all things are alive with purpose and intent, the potatoes in the bin at the grocer like a litter of pups, this one nudging to be picked by you, right now, while that one lays back waiting for another eye and hand. This is a world alive with courting and selections of the heart.

There is nothing in the world so seemingly insignificant or small that some other thing does not find it fascinating beyond measure. The style of each thing of the world includes its peculiar ability to hold the heart and mind of some other thing's interest. And just as the things of the world call to us and enliven our interests, their interest in us affirms our place in the world of things. What interests you, and what finds you of interest, is a showing of style that tells you where and how you belong. From this perspective, then, interest is the essence of community and relationships of all kinds. The things of the world offer countless places that our interests might call home, but over time we find that some places are more desirable and suitable to our style than others. Interest helps us to particularize our place in the context of things.

It helps to imagine interest as a thing in its own right; that is, interest cannot be reduced either to a thing's presence or to my feelings about the thing. From the perspective of style, the critical thing about interest is that it acts on its own accord. The word interest itself means to be in between, and so interest cannot properly be located either in me or in the thing to which I am drawn. Interest arises between the thing and me, providing common ground for mutual perception and appreciation. Think of how we gaze into that mysterious middle range when we ponder or daydream, our eyes open and focused on the in-between place between us and our ideas or dreams. This middle ground where things meet and come to know one another is made by interest.

We can imagine interest as a free-flying agent with interests of its own, like love itself. It pleases interest that it can facilitate the things of the world, drawing them to one another, allowing responses that ride on its willing back. Interest is the love inherent in between the things of the world, and, like love, interest exists beyond the reach of will. We cannot help that in which we are interested, and we cannot preclude the honest interest of others no matter how hard we might try.

Think how often the things of the world unexpectedly ignite passions in us of which we were previously unaware. You were a normal person until yesterday when you drove by a car lot and saw that blue convertible for sale. Now you are an idiot babbling about wire wheels and chrome. You skip lunch just to drive back by for another look, knowing in your heart that the car will still be there because where else could it be? It is so clear that you and the car are meant for each other that it is unthinkable to you that the car would let itself be taken by another. Such are the distracting and attracting powers of interest.

Interest is like a matrix of love that permeates the world of things and creates the opportunity for bonds between them. Interest makes the right combinations right, thereby creating a fertile context for introductions. Interest helps to particularize imagination through the mutual desires and desirability of particular things. It is not just anything that turns us on, but some particular things. This focusing of interest is essential to style, but it cannot be forced any more than love can be forced. Interests sort themselves out over time, and can live in many different places while they do the sorting. A thing's interests can carry it to a life of travel and wide-ranging exploration, or they can lead to the quiet solitude of a darkened den where explorations of another sort might occur. Or they can carry the thing to both places over time, now roaming, now retreating, now roaming in retreat, now retreating in the roam. From the perspective of style the point is not to predict where interests will take us but to follow them, trusting that they hold the promise of a welcoming world.

Like all things, interest has multiple potentials and meanings. We have so far seen two of these meanings. Interest can be the ability of a thing to draw the attention of others, like the power of the blue convertible that catches the eye meant to see it. And interest can refer to the feeling of having one's attention drawn to a thing, as when the collector professes an interest in his coins. But interest also has another range of meanings. Interest can refer to a right or share in something, as when one has an interest in a business concern. And it can be something of value given in return for the use of something else, as in interest paid on a loan or interest earned on an investment.

These last two meanings are never far from the first two. Indeed from the perspective of style it is best to assume that all of the potential meanings of a thing are always present whenever the thing is present. Although one particular meaning might be the intended and most applicable one given the context, the other meanings are always still there in the wings. A thing, then, always retains all of its meanings, including those that we now might consider archaic or obsolete. Context then suggests the most appropriate meaning for a given situation. This is much how the gods were imagined in times past, always present even when absent, each godly power always relevant and influential even though different contexts naturally accentuate some gods over others. The multiple meanings of a thing are always present just like the multiple gods are always present. No one meaning can exist without the simultaneous invisible influences of all the others. Absence, as we saw earlier, has presence, and so absent things may influence our interests.

We have said that interest refers both to the attractive quality of a thing and to our attraction to the thing. This interdependence and reciprocity of interest gains further nuance, depth, and precision in the context of interest taken as the holding of mutual shares. I might have an interest in a business concern, but that means the business also has an interest in me. Similarly, if I make an interest payment on money borrowed I get something and the lender gets something. Mutuality, in other words, and the idea of joint possibilities based on interest, lie at the heart of interest.

The idea that to be interested in something is to share in it harkens to ideas we have already seen. Interest as sharing in the things of the world is another way of looking at interest as that which makes community and relationship of all forms possible. Sharing evokes images of heart-felt concern, and so we can see interest as leading us to the things that most want and need our attention, thereby also indicating for us a place and purpose. Interest puts out the welcome mat, opening onto a wide world of things that both beckon and come calling. Some things seek us out among all other things while we are drawn irresistibly to others. Such are the ways of interest.

For style, all of the various meanings of interest are present together and so are taken as necessarily implicating one another. They co-exist and provide mutual support. So, for example, if I say I am interested in sailing I might mean that I find sailing interesting. But I also am saying, whether I knowingly intend to or not, that sailing is interesting in itself, that I am invested in sailing and it in me, and that sailing and I hold common shares in the interest between us. Sailing and I have a thing for one another, we might say, pointing to the intermediate world of interest that exists between sailing and me. It is as if sailing and I are on loan to one another; each providing something of great value to the other in return for good faith and like favors. Our mutual interest makes things possible for both sailing and me that otherwise would not be possible, and thereby also expands possibilities for the world of things in general and the world of interest itself, enriching all things the way honestly smiling people create an atmosphere of trust and opportunity. The inherent multiplicity of meanings present in all things is one of the things that make them so interesting. And because these meanings all co-exist, if we leave something out or add something new then everything changes.

———

A fox suddenly appears in my suburban backyard and my breath catches in my throat. I have only seen photographs and representations of foxes, and the sheer beauty of the actual animal rivets my attention. I am enthralled and watch closely as the fox prances its stiff-legged gait along the back fence. I am anxious for the fox to stay in view, wanting to see all of it I can, but I'm afraid that if I move too quickly to angle for a better look the fox will see me and be gone.

The fox is incredibly interesting. Its presence is palpable and its appearance here in an environment that I have come to think of as domestic and settled is almost surreal in its intensity. What is this fox doing here in the suburbs? Where does it live? What does it eat? How does it survive amidst concrete and cars? Look how it sits! Right there in the middle of the backyard it has sat down and is grooming itself. I can't move. The fox looks up and I could swear it is looking straight at me, but the reflected light off the windows probably hides me. Now the fox moves again, loping out of sight behind the garage.

For style, what matters most is that I keep my interest on what's interesting—namely the fox. My interest in the fox can take many forms according to what the fox shows me. The fox might reveal itself to me as to a naturalist, making me reach for binoculars and note pad. Just look at the minute and exquisite detail of its glistening coat and flashing eyes. Watch that big bushy red tail wave with its white circle and black tip fresh from an inkwell. Notes and sketches are made as the fox pulls me into its details.

Or perhaps, as in other times and places, the fox appears as an omen. Under this manner of seeing we still watch the fox carefully but with an additional interest in what it portends, its every action an augury indicating the shape of things to come. Here the fox becomes an epiphany that can be appreciated only to the extent that we are able to appreciate the fox in its finest detail. From the perspective of style, not only the devil but all gods reside in the details of things. Indeed for style there are nothing but details, overviews and generalities being left to the transcending mind. And so style insists that we become devoted to the accuracy of our viewing lest we misread what we are being shown. Just when, where, and how did the fox appear? What other things were around, or not, at the time? What was going on when the fox showed up? What happened then? What did the fox do, exactly? What invisibles came along with the fox or perhaps even sent it here to this place at this time? How did its appearance influence the context of things? Such might be the kinds of questions called forth by the fox. But please note that each of these questions maintains its focus on the appearance of the fox.

Contrast this manner of interest in the fox with the common mistakes of self-interest and symbolism where the fox is used as an opportunity to think about something else. Interest in the fox holds us to the fox, requiring that our perceptions, ideas, and questions remain centered on the fox in my backyard. If I choose instead to see the fox in terms of its relevance to me then I will lose the fox because I have diverted my interest from it to me. This misplacing of interest can also happen when instead of trusting the impressions made by the fox and allowing these impressions to instruct me about its nature I consider these impressions to be the result of my projections onto the fox. Then when I look at the fox all I see are allusions (illusions?) to my nature (I am foxy, or sneaky like a fox, or feel hounded like a fox). This usurpation of the fox by self-interest blinds me to the particular style of this particular fox and is an affront to the fox. We need only think of a time in our own lives when someone has been interested in us only for what we could be or do for them. Did we feel seen and appreciated? Were we encouraged to reveal more about ourselves? Self-interest precludes interest in the other things of the world, erecting a mirror where once there was a window.

In the world of this book, the fox, and only the fox, can educate our interest. This most emphatically does not mean, however, that there is only one proper way of being interested in the fox. The fox, like every other thing of the world, is interesting across a wide range of possibilities. The important thing from the perspective of style is to make sure that our interest stays with the fox and does not turn to ourselves. The goal is not to get it right in some absolute way but simply to try to do right by the fox. A clue to our success in this regard will be the effect our interest has on the fox. If we are interested in the fox in its own right then our interest will open opportunities for the fox that would not be there otherwise. Under these circumstances, the fox becomes more of itself as we watch and imagine. On the other hand, if my interest in the fox is intended to open opportunities for me (self knowledge, for example), then my interest is not really in the fox but in me; interest degenerates to self-interest.

Abstraction and symbolism similarly misdirect our interest from the fox that has now reappeared from behind the garage and is sniffing around an area of the yard where only a few days ago I saw a rabbit taking a nap. What is it about that area of the yard, I wonder, that attracted the rabbit and this fox? If I lose the fascination of such questions by dissolving my interest into foxes in general or the meaning of foxes as symbols that represent other things then once again I have turned my back on the fox. From the perspective of style the abstract or symbolic fox tells me next to nothing about the style of this particular fox. In short, from the perspective of style there is no interpretation, explanation, definition, or personal opinion about foxes or foxiness that is remotely as interesting and vital as that svelte red presence that just leapt over the bushes, one last flash of its bulls-eye tail and now gone.

What is true of the fox is true of all things of the world. Each thing appears to and impresses itself on our imaginations in its own unique, irreducible, and nonrepeatable way. In the world of this book we could not feel as we do without the things of the world that make these feelings possible. To imagine otherwise leaves us unable to distinguish the impressions both made and called forth by the things of the world from feelings and projections based on our self-interest. It is not that our feelings toward the things of the world are unimportant, quite the contrary. But from the perspective of style we must remember that our feelings about things are only trustworthy to the extent they increase our appreciation of things and not ourselves.

With this idea in mind we return again to the now departed fox. If I try to do right by the fox, making sure my interest is guided by the fox and its specific context then I can trust this interest as saying something significant about the fox. Under this view, then, if I see sadness in the fox's eye this would not necessarily be a projection or anthropomorphism on my part. Rather my perception of sadness in the fox would enlarge and deepen the world of the fox and my appreciation of that world. Sad about what, I might wonder.

Just as it is important to make sure our interest is directed toward the things of the world, it also is important to distinguish between what is interesting about a thing and what a thing's interests are. These two things do not necessarily coincide, that is, what is interesting about a thing does not have to include what the thing's interests are. Two people can have vastly different interests from one another, for example, but still find each other fascinating for a lifetime and beyond. The nuclear scientist renowned for his brilliance can be mostly interesting to his friends for other reasons. To a fishing buddy maybe what is most interesting are the scientist's many opinions about fish and fishing, or the way he always swears with innocent optimism by the newest jig in his tackle box. To a proud pastor perhaps what is most interesting about the scientist is his easy fidelity to his god in the midst of academic cynicism and celebrity. There are always many sides to things.

Interest enlivens the world of presence with the potential for desire and satisfaction. As we move through the world we encounter things that spark our interest. If we are governed by this interest, and keep it focused on the things that have given it rise, we find that we become more careful and inquisitive in our attitude toward all things. It is a great mystery that you and I can stand side by side before a thing and you will see much while I see little. This suggests that both you and I are necessary for the weave of the world, you the warp and me the weft in the presence of this thing and now vice versa in the presence of another. Interest requires all of the things of the world to attend to one another, helping each thing of the world to find its place among the rest.

Not only the cat is made by its curiosity. Obsolete meanings of curious include carefully or skillfully attended to, and the paying of fastidious attention to detail, intricacy, and subtlety. These meanings might be obsolete but they are not gone, and so curiosities teach us how to be curious, refining our interest. A thing captures our interest and we are drawn to it, our curiosity leading us further into its details, stoking our desire to know more as we poke and turn and sniff. We cannot get enough because interest is fathomless; there is always more to fascinate those who are fascinated. Sometimes interest can even put us at risk, pulling us beyond the usual and comforting to the exceptional and trying. But what are we to do, we curious creatures? No doubt curiosity can kill the cat, but then there can be no cats without curiosity.

CHAPTER THREE

Response

As the things of the world are drawn together through interest they respond to each other in countless ways. Although I can try to sit perfectly still while I watch the fox, I am ablaze with responses. Emotions, feelings, ideas, songs, images, twitching hands and feet, heart a-beating, eyes straining—numerous responses accompany the fox. And not only I have such responses. All of the things that make up the fox's context are also alive with response, just as the fox, too, responds as it moves among the things of the world with sure nose and quick feet.

From the perspective of style, responses are things in their own right and not merely results. The fox moves among the things of the world and those things respond to the fox's presence. It is true that without the fox these particular responses would not occur, but it is also true that the fox could not be what it is and move among the things of the world precisely as it does without these supporting responses preparing and providing the way. Style keeps the fox and the responses that contribute to it together as they are initially presented, and takes their mutual appearance to mean they are mutually necessary.

Keeping the fox and its context together is critical for appreciating style. A different approach, one that bypasses style, is to analyze the fox and its context, separating them from one another and postulating causal relationships and temporal progressions (first this then that). But this approach misses the mark because it eviscerates the presence of the fox by isolating it from its appearance and context. Worse, it subjugates the fox's context to the fox, as if the fox were the only active participant in its appearance. I am beholden to the fox for the gifts it brings, yes, but I also am necessary for the fox to be the fox that is capable of giving these gifts. Style provides a way of keeping the fox and me together in the manner we were presented; analysis and explanation tend to divide the house where the fox and I live, leaving matters of style to fall unattended.

We have to be careful not to separate things from their context when talking about response. This is especially difficult when response is paired indiscriminately to the idea of stimulus. The pairing of stimulus/response, with volition falling squarely on the side of stimulus, has divisive tendencies that reduce response to a "then" waiting for an "if." In the world of style, however, it is never clear which is which, stimulus or response, and the very imposition of such a choice is itself suspect. Such a scheme begs the question of how two separate things can interact if there is not already something between them. After all, there can be no stimulus without response as surely as there can be no response without stimulus. If so, then do such labels really matter? What matters is the fox.

The "/" that both divides and holds together stimulus/response bespeaks the in-between place of interest. Now we can connect the embedded responsiveness of the world to this in-between place, imagining that responses are manifestations of interest that give particularity to how the things of the world reach out to one another. The stray dog in the alley is immediately interesting and interested, but only through our mutual responses can we each discern the nature of our relative interests and know what to do. Does he lower and growl or show a tentative wag of tail? Do I beckon with open palm or shoo with back of hand?

Responses shape as they are shaped, no longer a matter of first stimulus then response but rather nothing but responses. For style, presence includes responsiveness, and vice versa. Each thing of the world comes complete with the ability to respond as no other thing can to the other things of the world. This unique responsiveness in turn makes the world possible in ways that would not otherwise be possible. In this world there is give and take in every gesture, call and response in every sound. This is a world alive with posture and song.

Response need not be limited to its pairing with stimulus. Even in psychology, which as a rule accepts the pairing of stimulus/response, there are theories about response that are more in keeping with our interest in style. The theory of affordances, for example, suggests that the things of the world are able to move among the other things of the world because these other things afford them this possibility. According to this theory, the squirrel knows how to jump for the branch because the branch affords the squirrel this knowledge — if no branch then no jumping and no squirrel. At the same time, the squirrel affords possibilities for the branch, making it a possible place for landing and thereby expanding its potentials within the world.

This theory has nice implications for style. We can imagine the world as a supporting and supportive place, affording opportunities for varied existence and experience. Our responses, then, cannot be separated from the world but rather contribute to it, are an essential part of it, supporting as they are supported, encouraging as they are encouraged. Our responses to a thing can never be isolated from it's responses to us, so to educate our responses we must learn to discern among them without ever being quite sure whose responses they are. From the perspective of style, all responses are communal acts.

When thinking about response it is important not to confuse the actual experience of something with our ability to explain the experience. Such explanations tend to impose a linear scheme on something that did not occur in a linear way. We then begin to string things out in our minds, suggesting a causality of events not given with the original experience. Once trapped in such thinking we are left chasing our tails, postulating now this then that as the proximate stimulus to my response while never knowing when or how to stop our analysis. There is always another "before" in the world of cause and effect, always another lead to track down.

The world of style maintains things in the manner they are presented, complete with context. Take the pin and the finger. We can call the sticking pin the stimulus and the withdrawn finger the response and be done with it. Or we can look more closely. Does not the particular way the finger suddenly recoils from the tip of the pin teach us something about the natures of both pin and finger? Perhaps this is the first time the pin ever stuck anything. If so then presumably it can learn much about the nature of things from its encounter with the finger. The finger affords the pin the possibility of sticking, we might say; the vulnerability of flesh offering different opportunities for the pin than that of taut balloon or tough canvas. Through such encounters the pin both learns and teaches about its capabilities and limitations and those of finger, balloon, and canvas. For style, stimulus and response, like appearance and perception, are two words for the same experience. We cannot separate the pushing pin from the coaxing resistance it meets in the other things of the world. All are present so all are necessary.

Response literally means to promise back. The "sponse" part of the word has the same roots as the word "sponsor," suggesting that response provides the opportunity for sponsorship. This idea is basic to style: the things of the world sponsor each other. They vouch for each other's integrity, acknowledging the wherewithal of all things and contributing, each of them, to the possibilities inherent in the other things of the world. Each response, then, is a return promise made to an equally promising world that by its very appearance pledges its support. Even resistance and rejection—such as that between pin and finger—are indications that each thing has a place among the other things of the world.

Responses help to place us and to move us among the other things of the world by encouraging our participation and holding forth the promises of mutual possibilities. Response therefore cannot be separated from responsibility. If the things of the world depend on the responses of the other things of the world, then it is incumbent on all things to be responsible in their responses. Responses are responsible both for things and to things. Responsible for things in the sense that responses make the things of the world possible; responsible to them for the same reason. Style says that I owe a duty to respond appropriately to the things of the world whose responses, after all, support me.

From the perspective of style, responsible responses maintain their focus and devotion on the things of the world. The most common mistake in this regard is once again the problem of self-interest. If my responses are intended solely to make things better for me at the expense of another thing then they are not responsible and I have contributed and learned nothing. Self-interest taints my sponsorship of things, offering promises with strings attached. If, for example, we explain our responses to the intelligence and soulfulness we feel in the other things of the world as our own projections being reflected back to us, then we miss the opportunities afforded by the other things of the world in their own right. Moreover, our feelings can then no longer be trusted to say anything significant about the world because they are not directed toward the world, which is assumed to be blank and uninteresting.

Such might be the case in other worlds where only people are granted presence, interest, and response, but that is not the world of this book. In the world of this book all things are taken as vibrant presences that are both interesting and interested, responsive places responsible to and for the other things of the world. In this world, for example, buildings take note of what and who crosses their thresholds. Buildings are taken as presences in their own right, not idle bystanders but active participants in community life, each with its own preferences and ideas. And so if we find certain buildings uncomfortable we cannot know for sure where this discomfort belongs. Is the building itself displeased about something? Maybe even sad or sick? Or do we close off such possibilities and explain away our breathlessness when within its walls as only another one of our panic attacks, dismissing the feelings we have about the building's presence as mere figments of our imagination? Surely the headache I get when I go inside the building is the result of my stress and secret worries. Surely I could not be experiencing what it feels like to be inside the building's sadness, pressed upon by frustrated walls. Surely there are no ghosts and buildings have no memories.

In the world of style there can be great forces in small things. We need only think of some small thing that is special to us to know this is so. From the perspective of style the responses you feel from and for grandfather's watch are testaments to the watch's presence as a carrier of unique power, memory, and significance. Only the watch can give you the feelings you get from it. We don't know why the watch doesn't give these feelings to other people; that is a private matter for the watch to decide. Perhaps it doesn't like the way someone else holds it or examines it with an eye toward value and resale. Or perhaps it knows that only those who have imagined together can share old times.

In any event, your responses will miss the mark if they are driven by concerns about something other than the watch. You might instead respond to the watch with a desire to attend to it more carefully and to make the world a better place for the watch. You also might draw closer to the watch, but that ultimately is between you and the watch. But if you confuse the feelings that the watch gives to you with feelings about what the watch means to you or how much it will fetch at auction then you will lose the watch before another second ticks away.

In closing this chapter we return to the pairing of stimulus and response for another look. We have seen that for style response lives in the tips of pins and fingers. It is as if response lives in and through the skin of things, so constantly alive and active that we take this constant aliveness as steadfastness and stability. The constant life of response goes unnoticed, much as we grow accustomed to the creaks and groans of an old house, or tune out the roar of airplanes on their flight path overhead. Response is ubiquitous, like the atoms and molecules we are told vibrate existence. In such a world, a stimulus of course stimulates. It excites, encourages, incites, invigorates, goads to action. But style insists that stimulus is not the only animating force present when stimulus meets and engages the things of the world. Response, too, is already there, calling and seducing and making stimulation possible.

The pairing of stimulus and response can therefore be seen as one of the many ways in which response shows itself, that is, it is an indication of how style proclaims response. The very willingness with which response accepts its second-billed status is significant, pointing perhaps to the charitable aspects of response that we have already seen present in its open call to sponsorship and responsibility. There is something significant in how response directs attention back to the stimulus—look at the pin, says the recoiling finger, pay attention to the building, says our aching head.

Response teaches by example that what matters most are the things of the world. Response constantly calls our attention to these things, urging us to respond, to mix it up, to reach out, and occasionally even to get burned. Call the things of the world stimuli if you wish, says response, but get out there. The only thing that response seems to ask is that we be responsible in our sponsorship of other things.

Just as imagination makes perception possible, it also enlivens the world of response. Every response of whatever kind is first an image and is influenced by the images that have and hold us. This is one of style's gifts, that we can learn from the responses of others about the imagination engendered by our presence. The greater part of our presence is always beyond us, residing in the interest and responses that the things of the world show in and to us. Without their imagination we could not be. And so the exchange of imagination present in the responses of the things is critical to reading and appreciating the styles of things. Unless we learn to read and heed the responses of the other things of the world as images and in terms of images then we will remain blind to style, both that of others as well as our own.

CHAPTER FOUR

Affinity

Our last introductory idea to the world of style is affinity, the peculiar attraction of certain things to certain things. We have seen that the things of the world appear as presences before the other things of the world and that each thing is vastly interesting and interested. And we have seen that each thing is alive with response. But things do not spark attention and enliven response equally among all other things. Interest and response are not homogenous; they are particular, finicky, and eclectic. The things of the world are choosy, or appear to be, constantly choosing this over that even as others single them out for special attention. But about one thing there is no choice—there is no denying desire.

Life comprises preferences and inclinations, our predilections given like the color of our eyes and as surely seen by the other things of the world. We can neither help nor hide our likes and dislikes, nor explain why we can do and enjoy some things and not others. Why can we only understand some things and not others? Why does our attention return again and again to similar themes and things? Why can we read and relish certain authors while finding others impenetrable? Why can one person not pay a dog to come to him while they rush uncalled to someone else? Why can one person hear Bach while another cannot? If I say that I have never liked spinach do I mean that this dislike was there from my beginning, given with me? For you mountains, for me beaches. French vanilla for some, butter pecan for others. We are not responsible for creating such preferences, but we are responsible to them as they lead us through a world of plenty to the things we like and do best.

It is important to place affinities carefully. Like interest and response, affinities exist in-between things. It is tempting to say that affinities exist within us because we feel so intimately the emotions that accompany them. But the greater parts of our affinities are found in the interaction of the many things of the world. It is as if affinities are unformed potentials given with the presence of each thing, and that as each thing encounters the other things of the world interest and response begin to call out and educate these potentials, leading each thing through the world according to its desires. One day boy meets piano and a prodigy is born. But please note that from the perspective of style there can be no pianists without pianos as surely as there can be no pianos without pianists. Affinity draws these necessary partners together to form a necessary partnership, holding them close and educating their possibilities. The affinity between boy and piano is exactly that—between the two, and it appears only with their coming together. The things of the world depend on each other to reveal the affinities that hold them together and give them particularity and place. Affinity, then, is the promise of experience and education.

When affinity gives us a special connection with a thing, our attitude toward that thing changes. Affinity gives rise to affection. Interest intensifies as we desire to know more and more about our new partner. Love interests we call them sometimes, affairs of the heart pertaining to significant others. Our responses, too, become more significant, and we craft them more carefully as intimacy grows and we strive to give our partner its best due. In general we find in our affinities that we simply can't get enough of playing the piano, or eating at our favorite restaurant, or reading our favorite novelist for the umpteenth time. In terms of style, then, affinities are neither abstract forms nor subjective feelings but appear only in and through the interaction of the things of the world.

The dictionary gives two general meanings for affinity. The first meaning echoes what we have just said, referring to a close relationship between things, especially by marriage (an "affine" is a relative by marriage). The second meaning, belonging to the natural sciences and chemistry, refers to structural likenesses among things. In biology, this second meaning takes the form especially of phylogenetic likenesses that arise within a common evolutionary scheme. In chemistry, this second meaning of affinity refers to the force that holds atoms together in chemical compounds.

The second meaning is in some ways more mysterious than the first, if mystery may have degrees. The idea that affinities appear among like structures is a nice one for style, as if some things suit each other because of affinities long in the making. Many of us have stood open-mouthed before old family photographs, finding the same nose on eight relatives over five generations. There is something of them in me, we think, and we don't even know it. And we don't. Such affinities seem to be better seen by someone else standing open-mouthed before old family photographs, finding the same nose on nine relatives over seven generations and touching your face with their finger, counting you in the mix.

What is true of noses is true of all things. There is no aspect of anything that does not bear ancestral and prehistoric markings, whether or not we recognize them as such. In the world of style newness abounds but little is lost. Affinity goes beyond family line to implicate our evolutionary essences. Affinity suggests that not only do we like our affines in the sense of enjoying them, but we also are like them in that we share structural likenesses reaching beyond history. Although affinities are always unique they often feel long in preparation, the way new lovers claim to have known each other always. Affinity therefore connects our styles with their evolutionary heritage, but here evolution no longer is seen as arising from a struggle for survival but from loving interactions devoted to the possibilities of style. In the world of this book, survival serves style by perpetuating the possibilities of display.

Chemistry takes us into similar uncharted territory. Here affinity exists at the most basic levels of physical reality as an invisible force holding together certain atoms to make possible particular chemical compounds. Again, affinity appears only when things come together. But not just any two atoms can be held together in such a fashion. Some respond willingly, some require more complex procedures, and some simply will not hold. Even in the world of chemistry, presumably ruled by natural law, affinity shows its fickle side, existing here but not there.

These scientific meanings place affinity at the heart of the natural world. Indeed it is affinity that makes the natural world possible by drawing particular things to one another and holding them close. Like a natural force, affinity makes the things of the world gravitate to one another in particular ways. And, like other natural forces, affinity is egalitarian in bestowing upon each thing the power to engage and be engaged. Affinity allows unique affections to blossom as each thing encounters the other things of the world.

A true story, recounted by James Hillman in his wonderful book, *The Soul's Code*. A four-year old girl hears a cellist playing a song on the radio and exclaims to her parents, "I want the thing that makes that noise." Thus is an affinity revealed, this time tinged with genius. The little girl goes on to be Jacqueline du Pré, one of the world's most gifted cellists. From the perspective of style, what is striking about this story is that girl and cello recognized one another when they encountered one another. Just think about the precision and particularity of this mutual recognition. All of those other noises on the radio. All of those other musical instruments. All of those other little girls. And out of all of that, this connection, immediate, forceful, and everlasting. As if girl and cello shared a common evolution waiting for this moment. As if their affinity found its way into every atom of their being to hold them together by a force beyond imagination, a force that encouraged the demand "I want the thing that makes that noise."

This sweet proposal takes us back to the first general meaning of affinity as close relationship, especially by marriage. The idea that affinity, like marriage, leads to public declarations of affection and devotion comports well with style. It suggests that affinities want to be acknowledged before the other things of the world. Perhaps this is because affinities are communal by their natures— it takes both little Jacqueline and the cello—and so naturally they want this communal nature reflected in the act of going public. Or maybe, like marriage, affinities give rise to third things existing between partners, public possibilities made possible through mutual devotion and intimacy. It is a testament to their affinity that the music made possible by the marriage between Madame du Pré and the cello surpassed anything that either might have done alone.

Like affinity, marriage echoes with forever. Marriage partners often feel as if they had just been waiting for each other to come along, two wanderers on separate paths until crossed by stars and destiny. And, like affinity, marriage begins with engagement as we declare ourselves to the other things of the world and begin to prepare for the possibilities inherent in coming together. I can think of no one else, says the engaged mind; I can feel you in every part of me beats the enraptured heart. These are accurate descriptions of how affinity feels.

But of course affinity, like marriage and all other things, answers to a fate beyond our understanding. From the perspective of style all beginnings and endings are shrouded in impenetrable mystery. Each thing comes into a world already underway. We cannot know why some affections blossom only for a season while others are perennial in persistence. We seem unable either to initiate or prolong their stay by an act of will. We cannot even be sure that they have left when they appear to have left. If absence makes the heart grow fonder then might we imagine that affinity is present in that absence, nurturing affection and sparking memory?

For our purposes, affinities are better tended to than guessed at. A woman chooses an appealing title off the shelf only to discover after reading a few pages that she read this same book forty years before. She had loved it then, but it had slipped away from memory over the years. Funny, she thinks, that she would choose it again now just as she had then. There's something about the title that appealed to her. And although she now reads with the added imagination of memory, and although the book can now speak to a more experienced ear, something of the old fling remains present, a phrase that ignites, or an image refreshing as morning dew.

The word affinity comes from a combination of old roots meaning near or bordering on. Connected meanings for affinity are related, akin, or neighboring. Like old books lingering on the shelf, these old meanings remain vibrant still.

We have seen that interest is not uniform among things, and that as an in-between place interest exists at the borders of things. And we have seen that borders vary in their length and character. Now we see that the old roots of affinity likewise point to borders. We share affinities like we share borders, neighboring closely with some things while remaining more distant from others. And, like borders, affinities are subject to change for reasons beyond our control. All we really can do is tend them, respecting the sovereignty and territory of other things while trying to be the neighbors we would like to have. Given the inherent volatility of borders, we do better to focus more on the act of bordering than on trying to predict future demarcations.

Like affinities, borders remind us that there are always multiple things present in proximity to one another. No matter how far-flung the outpost, there is no such thing as an isolated incident. And, like borders, affinities recognize and encourage the mutual integrity of things, an integrity demonstrated by the very fact of bordering. Good style and good sense carry forth this recognition, urging us to take each thing as it presents itself in its own place. There is much to be lost in overstepping one's boundaries, so affinities, like borders, require respect and may not be taken for granted. For style, then, the best borders are those trimmed with beauty, indicating through their design and maintenance where things come together nicely.

Affinity brings with it feelings of kinship, but style reminds us that this kinship is possible only through the accompanying presence of other things. For style, kinship is found only in kin. And so we must take great care in paying attention to the things of the world lest we miss the face of a relative in the crowd.

We saw earlier that interest and response both ask that we be responsible in our actions towards the other things of the world. Affinity adds particularity to these responsibilities by differentiating the things of the world for us, drawing us repeatedly to some things and not to others. Affinity teaches that we are most responsible to and for our affines. This does not mean that we are not also responsible to and for strangers or distant places, but only that affinity is adept at finding proper partners and providing needed focus. If everything does its proper job in answering the calls of its affines then all will be cared for so far as style is concerned. By revealing the love between things, affinity helps to shape the world according to best effect. Affinity asks that each thing do right by the things it loves. And it demonstrates that, in the world of style, there are no condemnations loud enough to shout down the small persistent voice that demands the thing that makes that noise.

In closing, a warning. Affinity cannot be dictated by will or circumscribed by fiat. Indeed affinities are not even things of our making or control. Affinities do not arise from our thoughts about the nature of things but rather are part of the unknowable mystery that makes thought possible in the first place. There can be no thinking without the mystery of affinity to allow one idea to be called forth by another. Affinities constantly surprise us with their associations, making the world a vibrant place through the endless combinations they encourage and make possible. There simply is no predicting which things will be drawn to one another. And there certainly is no way to mandate what affinities should or should not exist. All that can be said is that things inevitably will be attracted to the things that attract them. There is no denying desire.

AFFINITY

•

49

Part II

The Essentials of Style

Temperament

Taste

Talent

Tools

Teachers

Tradition

CHAPTER FIVE

Temperament

The essentials of style begin with temperament, an old word for an old idea. It is a word whose meaning has changed dramatically over time, and these changing meanings are especially instructive for our interest in style. The difference between how we commonly imagine temperament today and its older meanings point to radically different ways of imagining the many things of the world, and in particular the human's place among these many things. The older meaning of temperament accentuates the natural place of all things, including the human, in the cosmos. The more modern meaning of temperament separates the human from the greater cosmos and isolates us in a foreign world of things assumed to be essentially different from the human.

As originally used, "temperament" referred to a particular style of imagining the cosmos. Under this old view, it was imagined that the human was a combination of four humours (blood, phlegm, bile, and choler). A person's temperament was determined by the particular mixture (Latin *temperamentum*) of these humours. The various humours themselves bore distinctive qualities, and when mixed together these humours combined to determine a person's overall demeanor or manner. One mixture might result in a person with a dry, cold temperament while another mixture produced a warm, moist temperament. According to the mixture of humours that constituted a person, he or she might be of good temper or bad, possessed of good humour or ill. It all depended on the mix.

There was nothing more basic to a person, or to anything else for that matter, than temperament. In people temperament was assumed to be vastly influential on their tastes and talents, some temperaments suiting a person for some things but not others. Various theories were espoused along these lines, with people wondering then as now, for example, about the curious relationship between scholarly and artistic abilities and a melancholic temperament. Certain temperaments just seemed to prepare people better for some activities than others, even though such theories were, and are, constantly bedeviled by the many exceptions to their rule.

Temperament is a useful idea for style because it requires that we affirm things as they are. There is something nice in knowing that my fellow humans are all made from the same stuff as I am, only differently configured. This means, too, that I must accept and affirm all aspects of my temperament, the pleasing along with the not so pleasant.

Temperament gives life, but it also presages death and is perhaps the strongest impression left by a thing after its passing. In fact under the old view of temperament what we call diseases were referred to as "distempers." But not only disease was a result of the humours. A person's character, too, was imagined to result from the precise mixture of humours that a person comprised. The humours were responsible for all that we could be, both in sickness and in health. Temperament was seen as a gift from the gods themselves, and was therefore a testament to one's precise place in the cosmos. No two things could have the exact same temperament, but because all things were made of common stuff we were affirmed in our understanding of one another's natures.

It is especially important for style that temperament in these older times indicated that the human was part and parcel of the greater cosmos, a realization increasingly lost to more modern perspectives about the human. In the old world of temperament the human had not yet been split into categories of body and soul and was not imagined as essentially different from the other things of the world. Instead the human was seen alongside the other things of the world as all contributing to the greater cosmos. According to this view, the showing of a thing through style is a display of opportunity, showing not only what the humours were capable of producing in this thing, but holding out the possibility for communal action among like things.

What is critical to remember is that the humours that constituted the human did not belong only to the human but rather were gifts from the greater cosmos. Humans were the stuff of the cosmos, so to speak, not in a grandiose or inflated way, but in the mundane sense of simply being part of things. This view of the human as an integral and essential part of the greater world led to the old ideas of microcosm and macrocosm, with the human being imagined as the cosmos writ small. The stars and planets, for example, were imagined as exerting influence on the human because we shared their existence. Whatever reverberated in the greater world also echoed in the human.

Listen to Owen Barfield reconstruct this remarkable world:

> [T]he medieval scientist believed with Hippocrates that the arteries of the body were ducts through which there flowed, not blood, but three different kinds of *ether* (Greek "aither," "the upper air") or *spirits* (Latin "spiritus," "breath", "life"): ... the *animal* (Latin "anima", "soul"), the *vital*, and the *natural*. But the stars and the planets were also living bodies; they were composed of that "fifth essence" or *quintessence*, which was likewise latent in all terrestrial things, so that the character and the fate of men were determined by the *influences* (Latin "influere", "to flow in") which came from them. The Earth had its *atmosphere* (a kind of breath which it exhaled from itself); the Moon, which was regarded as a planet, had a special connection with *lunacy*, and according as the planet Jupiter, or Saturn, or Mercury was *predominant* or in the *ascendant* in the general *disposition* of stars at a man's birth he would be *jovial, saturnine,* or *mercurial*. Finally, things or persons which were susceptible to the same *influences*, or which *influenced* each other in this occult way, were said to be in *sympathy* or *sympathetic*. (*History in English Words*, page 142, italics in original.)

To give some small idea of how our perspectives about things pervade our thoughts and ideas we need only realize that all of the italicized words in the paragraph quoted above came into use during the time the world was imagined in this fashion. Imagine. Imagine how such words, and the ideas they grace, shape the world in which we live. Not only then but always. There are few things more revealing about a person's style than the words they use and the ideas they take for granted. Where we are sure about things may well tell more about the nature of our certainty than about things themselves.

We shift now to the seventeenth century, where a new view of the human has emerged. The French philosopher Descartes has declared *cogito ergo sum* ("I think, therefore I am"), and has thereby shifted the focus from the cosmos working in and through humans as natural constituents to one where the center of attention is the human person imagined as having an interior core separate from the rest of the things of the world. In keeping with this new view of the human, the words "self," and its hyphenated progeny ("self-confidence," "self-esteem," etc.), along with "ego," "egoism," and "consciousness" come into use and mind. Barfield calls this process of postulating an interior consciousness private to the human and then subsuming the world into this consciousness "internalization." Throughout this book we will see the process of internalization repeated again and again, always with bad results for style. It is, in many ways, the great curse of the modern mind.

When the human comes to be defined as essentially different from the greater cosmos the old idea of temperament is turned inside out. Where once temperament was an indication of how we belonged to the greater cosmos, now it is imagined as referring to something private to each person that is not connected in any significant way to the greater cosmos. The windows of the soul become one-way mirrors with the individual ego watching the world go by.

The old idea of temperament made sense of the sympathetic feelings that connect like things by suggesting they share similar dispositions given by similar humours and influences. Under the modern view the human is extracted from the greater cosmos and sympathies are reduced to anthropomorphic projections from a secret self that animates the things of world through thinking about them. By the eighteenth century everything has been turned on its head. The human now is imagined as an individual standing alone in a brute world run according to mechanical law. Only we are divine; the rest of things are simply there for our use and amusement. The word "outlook" first appears at this time in the sense of suggesting a detached and withdrawn ego looking out onto a world of essentially foreign things.

This little history in words is significant to style because style depends on the other things of the world for its existence and withers when deprived of these other things. As such, style is more closely aligned in terms of imagination with the older view of temperament than the newer one. Like the older view, style imagines that each thing is an influential and indispensable part of the greater world. And, like the older view, style imagines that things can be drawn together through their susceptibility to similar influences, like moving with like because they are carried by common currents. Moreover, such influences are not felt to come from an outer world apart from human interiority (outer and inner being ideas foreign to this perspective). Rather all things are seen as part and parcel of a cosmos through which influences flow.

When temperament is claimed as a possession of the self imagined in isolationist terms it loses its vital connections to the greater world of which it is a natural part and becomes a fraction of what it once was. Set adrift from its moorings among the other things of the world, temperament loses its direction and, over time, becomes off course and ill tempered. Style suffers. Where once temperament provided each thing with a stamp of uniqueness, and thereby ensured each thing of its place alongside the other things of the world, now temperament separates us from things, making each thing a prisoner of its own privacy.

But in the world of style the old meaning of temperament remains vibrant and is seen as a testament to one's indelible place in the world. In this world there is no clear distinction between in and out, both being matters of perspective, and there is no vantage point from which one can be said to have an outlook on a world apart from oneself. This view also reminds us that each thing is as it is and can be no other. In contrast to more modern views that suggest the human is capable of changing their essential natures through introspection and training, temperament says that whatever change is possible in a person's life will take place within the context of his or her temperament. Far from being blank slates, temperament says that each human is full of the raw materials he or she will need to live their lives.

By drawing our attention to what our temperaments allow, style helps to refine our perceptions of ourselves within a more limited, humble context. Nothing can do everything, and hyper-motivational views of the human saying that we can be whatever we want to be are misleading and, ultimately, disheartening. It is far better to know that temperament both grants and limits my abilities. The worth of each thing is then increased because its abilities are valued as offering perspectives and possibilities otherwise unavailable. The blessed limitations given by temperament are among style's most powerful gifts. They grant both challenge and comfort — challenge because they call upon us to craft a life out of what we are given, and comfort because we are no where more at home than in our temperament.

Style knows that each thing is limited in its awareness and potential and celebrates this knowledge as the nature of things. In the world of style each thing can do only what its temperament allows. In turn this reaffirms style's lesson that all things are needed to accomplish what can be accomplished. Style knows that untold and unseen influences are always at work, and so it is watchful for influences that ripple across the surfaces of things. So much can be learned from a simple gesture, the cosmos displayed in miniature through the style of things.

In the world of style, temperament helps to establish the particular presence of each thing in the world. At the same time it makes possible communication and understanding among things. No two mixtures can be exactly alike and yet sympathy, what we are calling affinity, persists in abundance among the many things of the world. There is nothing so odd that it is without partners. It is through our makeup, we might now say in an echo of the old idea of mixture, that we are drawn to the things to which we are drawn. And although we can perhaps learn to temper our temperament over time, refining what the cosmos has given, we cannot change the stars that bear us.

We must remember, however, that the temperament we perceive in other things cannot be reduced to type or category. Although temperament might predispose us to particular actions we can never be sure what something is capable of doing. Regardless of a thing's temperament, there simply are too many other unseen and unrecognized influences at play to support pat predictions. Temperament is too mysterious and too unknowable for us to categorize. Style is content simply to take things as they are without worrying too much about what comes next.

Although we tend to talk about a person's temperament as if it was one thing it is in fact essentially multiple and will over time show many facets. Temperament is a stylistic concern, after all, and so remains in the world of imagination and aesthetics, a world not subject to predictions based on hard and fast rules. Certainly we can have imaginings about the temperaments of other things, and through affinity perhaps even partake in the temperaments of like things, but such imaginings are always subject to many other influences beyond our awareness or comprehension. Style's main concern is to appreciate temperament as an aesthetic presence beyond definition or control, letting each thing show us its potentials according to its own lights. In the end it is probably best to be temperate in making too many declarations about temperament.

In the world of style, the time in which a thing exists is strongly influenced by temperament. Temperament connects each thing to a particular style of time. According to the temperaments involved, one person can wait five minutes in line and leave in a huff complaining of slow service while another person, after the same by-the-watch wait, takes a little extra time to complement the manager on the staff's speed and efficiency. Who is to say how long the wait? It does little good to tell the irate customer that it has been only five minutes because they certainly are going to take issue with that word "only." For them the wait was as it was experienced and no amount of so-called objective evidence can change that experience.

But the time given by one's temperament is more pervasive and profound than the length of one's fuse. Temperament is heart time, the rhythm that we feel in the world, the tapping of the unwatched foot, the breath as it comes and goes, and the years as they, too, come and go. Each thing lives its own beat. Style grooves to this beat.

And so a person's temperament will leave them out of time in some circumstances and in sync in others. Style expects such variations in time and does its best to take each thing in terms of the tempo the thing itself sets, like the surfer who sits upon his board watching the waves, getting into their rhythm. There is no rushing the big ones; they will come when they come. To be ready one must be in time.

The idea that temperament sets the times in which we live frees style from punching the clock. Gone are the pressures and anxieties of the here and now, of falling behind or getting too far ahead of ourselves. Instead style teaches us to expect variations in time as the due course of things. Style runs according to its own clock. This means that sometimes a thing can feel completely out of touch with the trappings of its age, but can do so without rancor or frustration. How many of us share temperaments better suited to other times? Such are the foibles of style, which is content to imagine that each thing lives time in its own way and that it shares this time with others of like temperament, whenever and wherever they occur. In the unimaginable space of time who can ever say what is truly offbeat?

Of course no thing can escape the time in which it lives. Our modern age provides the molds into which our temperaments are poured. But temperament also is cast of the eternal, teaching that each thing is both once and always. Temperament is completely contemporary even as it is a gift from beyond time, the temperament of each thing offering an example of how the cosmos takes care of its own each in its own time. And so we will sometimes presage the future in the out-of-date, or catch a glimpse of what is to come in our early morning mirrors. Temperament makes our first mark on the world, touching each nuance and subtlety, and, when all is said and done, it perhaps leaves our most lasting impression. Like the point of light that continues to hold its place in the constellation we behold at night long after the star, we are told, has blinked goodbye.

CHAPTER SIX

Taste

The second essential of style is taste. Like all essentials, taste is both given all at once with a thing even as it is capable of refining over time. It is taste that teaches us best about excitation and pleasure, both the quick and the long. If temperament is the relatively unrefined stuff of the cosmos as it appears in the style of a thing, then it is taste that refines and gives precision to that appearance. There is no other peach that tastes like this one, whether we judge it good or bad. It tastes as it tastes because it cannot taste any other way. If it did it would not be this peach.

Some tastes come and go—I might never have liked spinach until I was thirty, for example—but over time things settle into their tastes and are comforted by the things that please them. This settling in is especially important for style and is best revealed through a thing's tastes. In a sense this settling in is present in every experience and gives the experience its feeling of substance. Style takes things as they are settled in at any given time, and relies on taste to distinguish among various kinds of settling. Here is a settling in that tastes flat, says style; here is a settling in that tastes of integrity.

From the perspective of style it is best to take things as they appear with the assumption that they have always been so and always will be so. With ideas of explanation and change set aside we are better able to taste things in their own right. Of all the essentials of style, taste best teaches how to take each thing according to the flavors they bring to the table. At the same time, taste teaches us that our abilities to appreciate things are not uniform, we can appreciate some things better than others and some things not at all. Taste opens the world to exploration at the same time it gives direction and guidance, teaching each thing about its place in the world through its likes and dislikes. Inevitably some tastes are foreclosed to each thing. Try as I might I cannot learn to like liver and onions. Tastes are not acquired; tastes are received.

There is no explaining why things taste as they do or why my taste guides me to some things and not to others. A fabric that looks dreadful to me might be fawned over by you. There is no right or wrong in such cases, only difference. Taste affirms the necessity of differing sensibilities. It takes both me and you, we can imagine, to appreciate the various potentials offered by the fabric. My taste shows it as ugly; your taste sees it as beautiful.

This variety of tastes is sometimes devalued and passed off in terms of relativism—everyone has their own tastes and so there is no sure way to claim one thing good and another bad. But relativism exists only in the mind of relativism; it is the style of such thinking to see things in relativistic terms. We might even say that it suits relativism's taste to view things in such a manner. But relativism exists outside the immediacy of taste itself. From within the context of a thing's taste there can be no greater certainty about things. It is not a matter of opinion with me and liver and onions. My taste is quite certain.

Only from the abstracted perspective of relativism can the certainty given by my taste be diluted by claims that others taste differently. For style, taste is not subject to contradiction and can easily accommodate differing tastes. You can like liver and onions and I can dislike them, and we can both be sure in our tastes. Taste does not ask for agreement or depend on confirmation from outside taste itself.

Taste is not relative but rather gives proof that there are numerous tastes that are each certain within themselves. Taste is always particular, and no two tastes can ever be said to be the same. This is important for style because taste demonstrates quite clearly that each thing has its own particular tastes that can be trusted to tell us something specific about the world. At the same time, taste is obviously limited in each thing and so all things are required to fully savor the things of the world. Taste teaches that we can be sure about something without inflating our sureness into general claims about the nature of things. Neither you nor I can be said to be correct about that piece of fabric even though we are both quite sure in our tastes.

Taste is especially interesting because it always implicates more than one thing. In the world of style, there is always both the thing that impresses itself upon taste and taste that registers and appreciates this impression, both the tongue that tastes and the thing that tastes on the tongue. Taste reconfirms style's lesson that nothing exists in isolation. Indeed attempts to taste things in isolation can lead to extracts so potent and freakish in concentration that they can barely be tolerated, parodies of flavor no longer at home on the tongue. Gone is the roundness and complexity of the taste of things as they exist in the world of other things. Just think of how when we try to describe the taste of something we refer to the flavors of other things in an attempt to concoct a recipe on the tongue's imagination. This is yet a further example of how in the world of style all things implicate and depend on one another. There is no talking about the things of the world without the things of the world.

Taste can mean putting something in the mouth to try it, the particular liveliness of a flavor on the tongue, the preferences of a particular thing for some things over others, and a more general aesthetic judgment about the appropriateness of things. The first three meanings refer to nonreflective acts and are given with perception itself. Only the last meaning requires reflection. It takes no thinking on my part to know that I don't like liver and onions, but I cannot be so sure in my statements about what is in good taste or bad. Given this uncertainty, style tends to take appropriateness as a laudable ideal in itself while not trusting hard judgments about what is or is not appropriate.

By constantly emphasizing differentiation, taste helps to avoid the encrustations of ideology. My tastes give me a very precise take on things. At the same time, however, I am aware that others taste things differently. And so my tastes cannot be elevated to judgments about things in general but must always remain open to the tastes of other things.

Although taste is always a present experience it includes memory. One old idea about memory considered memory to be present imagination with past time added, and this is certainly so with the memory of taste. As the wine approaches the lips it excites imagination, taste already activated and anticipating what is to come. And as this particular wine is savored it also recalls other wines once enjoyed. Taste coalesces time by infusing memory and flavor with one another, thereby reminding us that there is no experience that does not carry the presence of things imagined as past. Psychologists tell us that taste, along with its highly influential partner smell, is especially adept at evoking memories beyond the reach of cognition. A taste of a certain pie and we are back home sitting at the kitchen table, toes scuffing the floor in delight.

Taste is something that the things of the world do together and so is an indicator of style. Yes we taste the orange by putting it in our mouths but the orange also is itself in action tasting like an orange and impressing itself upon our taste in a manner unlike all other things. And even among oranges this one tastes different from other ones to someone adept at tasting oranges. In the world of style, all things make impressions and are actors credited with their own volition and potentials. The world of style is an active place, and taste is one way this activity is revealed. We might taste the orange but not without the orange also making itself available to us and our tastes. Taste requires both the orange and us and cannot be located in one without the other.

It is a wonderful thing that taste both limits our abilities to perceive the other things of the world at the same time it intensifies that which we perceive. I might never be able to like liver and onions and so am foreclosed that particular blessing, but, on the other hand, I am privy to special information about my favorite enchiladas. Taste gives us example after example of the world in a teacup and suggests that it is not the accumulation of things that constitutes worldliness but the depth of our tastes.

In addition, taste shows us that there is variation within all things depending on their context. This particular wine will taste differently with fish than with beef and will similarly reveal nuances in each dish. My ability to taste, too, is affected by context. A pack of crackers and a can of sardines might taste great on a summer afternoon sail, but not be a first choice on a winter's evening spent by the fire.

If taste reveals the differences among things it also tends to associate things according to taste. Bacon and eggs, steak and potatoes—some tastes seem destined to join forces. Still other things seem to resist being put together no matter how hard we try. But even here taste resists absolutes. Rest assured that even if there is general agreement in the world of fashion that stripes and checks don't go together there will be someone somewhere who loves the look of the combination and who looks great wearing it.

This joining together of things according to taste is essential to style and begins to suggest an orderliness to things. Taste brings order to the cosmos by focusing interest and revealing affinities, and so the more our styles are guided by taste the more confident and coherent they become. We will see later on how traditions hold similar styles together, but for now we can say that taste is how we first experience this natural association of things. In the world of style some things accompany one another, like the side dishes that compliment and complete the main course.

Like the other essentials of style, taste is largely unavailable to introspection. Taste implicates an on-going engagement with the other things of the world and is found only in our experience of other things. For no apparent reason this child prefers the rough and tumble while that one reserves and studies. Taste leads us through the greater world according to what we have a nose for and what we can best appreciate. In turn, our taste educates us as to our possibilities by placing us within the contexts of things we can enjoy while steering us away from those we cannot. Through following our tastes we come to know what we like and dislike, and these lessons help to circumscribe our styles.

But more than anything else, taste indicates preferences and inclinations. Finding something to our tastes it is like finding a friend. Because taste always implicates more than one thing, we can never be quite sure where our preferences mostly lie. Does the sauce taste so good only because I like it or also because it likes me? That pizza last night didn't agree with me, we say, indicating that pizza, too, has its preferences. In the world of style such mutual possibilities are accepted. What matters is that the taste arises between me and the sauce and so is a receptacle for the preferences of both.

It is difficult to imagine taste without preference entering the picture. The word taste itself is thought to be a blending between two words: *tangere*, meaning touch, and *gustare*, meaning liking or relishing. The word gusto also comes from this latter word, referring to a fervor and zest for things. Curiously enough, *gusto* in Italian also refers to the style of a work of art. Style and taste seem to require one another and to both implicate aesthetic appreciation. Taste therefore naturally includes both discrimination and preference and is rarely satisfied with bland distinctions. Taste leaves little doubt about its likes and dislikes, making it clear that I will prefer some things over others and that some things will find me to their liking while others will not.

There is something comforting and encouraging to style about the refining powers of taste. For style, each thing of the world brings its own special tastes to the communal table. Each thing tastes the other things of the world in its own way and is tasted by the other things of the world in their own ways. There is room for everything in such a world, every taste finding a place to enjoy what it enjoys. In this world, I am responsible to my tastes even if I am not responsible for them. I don't know why I like enchiladas so much, but because I do it behooves me to seek out the best enchiladas I can find or make. My taste requires this of me. In the end, both enchiladas and my tastes are better for our joint efforts, both enriched by the gift of taste. And, what I might be able to do for enchiladas someone else can do for liver and onions. All are present and so all are necessary.

There is yet another reason why it is significant that taste is displayed through preferences and inclinations. Our ability to appreciate the other things of the world, and to make contributions to these other things, is dependent on our particular tastes. There is nothing impartial about taste. Taste provides us with our own peculiar slant on things by allowing us to experience things in a manner unlike any other thing. Taste reaffirms the necessity for multiple perspectives by showing that there are always multiple ways to taste anything. In this sense, all tastes are inherently biased. This is a critical idea for style. According to taste it is our biases, slants, leanings, and inclinations that matter most, and not those places where we are upright, straight, and conformed. Taste directs us to, and helps to define our oddness, and through taste we discover things that nurture this oddness.

Given the bias inherent in all taste it is best to be cautious in making blanket claims about what is or is not in good taste. Once we move beyond claims based on our own tastes we are on shaky ground. General claims about good and bad taste tend to become moralistic judgments based on a communal aesthetic about what is and is not appropriate. For style, it is best to tend to one's own tastes without trying to force them on others. Such forcing is pointless anyway. If a person does not agree with you about something being in bad taste you are unlikely to persuade them otherwise. Taste answers poorly to persuasion and can only really be influenced through other tastes.

The oldest meanings of taste referred to handling and exploring something by touch and feel. In Old French, the etymology of "taste" referred to a tool used to probe wounds. Might this suggest that through taste we enter openings presented to us by the things of the world?

Taste is where we touch and are touched. We might even imagine that taste includes the emotional meanings of these words. When our hearts are touched by a particular poem is it not taste that allows this contact beyond the incidental? Watch a collector handle her chosen objects and you will see her taste in her hands— see how she cradles and supports each thing, savoring it through touch and taste. Her style is much revealed here. Does this also suggest that we might learn to handle things better by better educating our tastes? Perhaps taste is a way to educate our feelings by keeping them in touch with the other things of the world. Perhaps this is a way of thinking about feeling that avoids the cataclysmic introversion we saw take place with temperament. Perhaps taste-based education would rely upon the other things of the world to help us develop our discerning abilities. Taste can learn only through tasting, after all, and like style loses something important when it shields itself with projections about the other things of the world. Taste replaces projection with anticipation, looking forward to that next bite.

Lastly, taste teaches something basic about quantity and quality. The word taste itself can refer to a small amount of something. A taste is a bit, a sip, a morsel, only a touch. If someone asks us to try a sauce we usually dip just the tip of the spoon. There are two times when we taste things this way. The first is when we try something for the first time. Here we take just a little taste in case we turn out not to like it. The other time we taste something like this is when we want to savor it. Here, too, we take just a little taste, but this time we do so that we might be especially appreciative in our tasting.

There is something about taking only a little bit that concentrates taste, as if taste itself refines to match the smallness of the portion received. A taste of something implies its essence, as when a guidebook offers a taste of Spain or the circumstances of life give a person a taste of one's own medicine. Taste seems to work best in moderation, taking only enough to be enjoyed. It is difficult to imagine taste in the context of gluttony. The sheer quantities indulged obliterate the delicacy required by taste.

Taste best informs style through countless small preferences, both those made and those received. The broad and extravagant rarely reveal as much about a thing's style as do the small choices it makes all the time according to taste. Style is best served, then, through abiding and honoring its tastes.

Given the importance of taste for style, it is no accident that affectation of style often proceeds through affectation of taste. And so there at that table in the center of the restaurant sits the wine snob, sniffing over his swirled glass, more interested in how others are perceiving his well-rehearsed routine than in the bouquet rising to meet his upturned nose. But such affectations cannot last; we cannot forever pretend to like what we don't like. Style depends on taste, and it is through the mutual education of taste by style and style by taste that both learn about the peculiar essence their own essentials.

CHAPTER SEVEN

Talent

If temperament reveals the cosmos in the style of a thing, and taste guides style through preferences and inclinations, then talent encourages things to do what they do best. There is no telling why different things are capable of doing what they can do. It is a mystery that one person touches a piano and is playing before you know it while another person just can't play the piano no matter how he tries. But where the piano stays out of his reach, this same person might be able to tune an engine or make a home or be a friend like nobody else. Talent defies explanation.

But for style what matters most is not why things do what they do but simply that they do what they do. Style wants to see what things can do. Style is interested in what happens and in the things that talent displays. Not to understand them, although understanding is one way of looking, but to be wowed by them, to see the extraordinary precision and beauty of talent fulfilled. At the same time, the style of each thing wants to show the other things of the world what it can do. Not by way of competition, although competition is one way of showing, but for the sheer joy of talent fulfilled.

What is more beautiful than watching something do well what it does best? A horse charging full tilt across a field, a rock holding its place, a painter mixing colors, a gardener tending beds. What is more pleasing and encouraging than accomplishing a project that calls upon one's talents with grace and competence? There are enormous powers at work in talent, powers that have the capacity to make things other than they currently are. Through talent style becomes an agent for opportunity and change.

The oldest meaning of talent was as a measurement of weight. It also referred to a monetary unit based on weight. It takes its modern meaning as an ability or aptitude from the New Testament parable of the talents (Matt. 25:14-30). In this parable, talent is a metaphor for a person's god-given predispositions, this person being adept at making money with money, for example, while that one is too timid to do the same. Moreover the parable suggests that person is destined to act according to his or her talents. It seems that talent must be obeyed as surely as God's commands.

Even apart from its biblical connotations, talent is often taken to mean an ability or aptitude received from sources other than the human will or conscious choice. We do not choose our talents but discover them. We can substitute genetics for God, but talent remains a mysterious gift from beyond our comprehension. Talent compels us to its service.

Talent shares the idea of being given by God with an older word, genius. In its earliest usage, genius referred to a tutelary spirit bestowed by the gods that gave a person his or her unique abilities. Genius was a godly presence, a divine incarnation felt as natural ability. As such, genius exerted extraordinary influence on a person and could even possess them. But it would have been nonsensical in those times to talk of someone as being a genius. Such terminology would have crossed the line between mortals and gods, equating the human with the divine.

The Greek word *daimone* carried much the same meaning as the Latin *genius*. It, too, was understood as a divine presence that bestowed special ability. And, like genius and talent, the *daimone* engaged this ability in the call of destiny. The *daimone* often was felt then, as now, as a special calling, a longing, a special devotion. *Daimones* came and went however they came and went, and there was little mortals could do except abide and honor them. They were essential to life; without them we were just dead people walking. Socrates, for example, perceived his *daimone* as a small voice that told him what not to do. It did not offer prospective or proactive advice but guided him through objections and warnings. He attributed whatever special ability or wisdom that possessed him to this voice. The word demon is derived from the Greek *daimone* but the evil and hellish associations of demon derive from early Christianity. The Greek word carried no such prejudice.

The idea that things receive their special abilities from divine sources shifts radically from about the seventeenth century onward, once again falling into the deforming hands of internalization. The meaning of genius, for example, suffers a similar shift in meaning as we saw earlier with the meaning of temperament. Genius, instead of being a divine presence working through a person, becomes an aspect of the person. Instead of genius possessing the person, the person comes to possess genius. Even more radically, the person becomes a genius, is said to *be* a genius. The line that once proscribed the sacred and the profane it crossed as person and genius are equated.

During this shift in meaning, genius was at times actually opposed to talent, the latter term doggedly hanging on to its meaning as something given and received from divine quarters. Even talent, though, has increasingly shown signs of being internalized in the same manner as genius. When we refer to a talented person as "the talent," for example, we see the same flip-flop of meaning that befell both temperament and genius. Under the traditional meanings of both genius and talent, a phrase like "the talent" would have been seen as downright blasphemous.

From the perspective of style, it is better to imagine talent as something received to which we owe fealty and responsible action. Internalizing talent takes talent away from where it actually appears and acts among the other things of the world. If talent is made part of me, and considered to be for my personal benefit and self-expression, then I begin to view the other things of the world as relevant only insofar as they address these personal wishes and concerns. I begin to spend large amounts of time and energy trying to figure out where my talent came from and what it says about me. On the other hand, if talent is something given to me from divine quarters, then I am obligated to direct my attention to fulfilling *its* needs and requirements. I then begin to spend large amounts of time practicing and improving the talents I have been given so I might realize their goals and aspirations. I am excited by what these talents can do, and am glad to see the beautiful and pleasing things they can contribute to the greater world. Internalizing talent begins the inward spiral of introspection, leading me and the talents I have received away from the other things of the world. Addressing talent as a responsibility I owe to the divine leads to public action as talent follows its irrepressible desire to get to work.

It is common to hear people complain about not being fulfilled or satisfied by one's work. We now can see that such complaints derive much of their distracting power from the internalization of talent. From the perspective of style, complaining that one's work is not satisfying to the worker puts the emphasis on the wrong place. Style is more concerned with satisfying one's work and fulfilling its needs. Talent doesn't seem really to care much one way or the other about personal concerns, opinions, or well-being. The painting is more important than the painter's feelings and opinions about the painting, which, from the perspective of style, have no more standing than any other person who has feelings and opinions about the painting. For talent, what is at issue is doing right by the talents one has been given. If these talents are honored to the best of one's abilities then all that can be done has been done.

There often can be tensions between one's personal wishes and the demands of one's talents; taste and talent are not always in agreement. There are lots of talented art critics who can't draw and lots of talented painters with dubious taste. This tension is felt quite objectively, if that is the right word, as existing between different things each having their own volitions and concerns. Older styles of imagining this tension would have seen it in terms of the ongoing tension between mortal concerns and the wishes of divine necessity. Under these older views sacrifice is to be expected when answering one's talents. By their very natures (divine), talents pull us beyond our capabilities, always asking that we strive to match their beauty and perfection. Then life is seen as an on-going devotion in the service of talent, and talent becomes an indication of what the gods have in mind for us.

This tension also perhaps suggests a more private side to taste that is uncomfortable with talent, which is inevitably public. As a divine gift, talent says that even what appears to be the solitary practice of one's talents is brimming with communal influences and interaction. Witness the seeming solitude of Emily Dickinson, her poems resting quietly in a drawer all those years, waiting for their public life to begin. But to recognize the public aspect of talent we must cast our idea of the public wide enough to include the presence of the many things of the world. The writer is never alone, even if no other person is in the room. As the writer struggles for the right word he or she calls upon any number of assistants and is bedeviled by any number of gadflies. The dictionary has no answers, but the view out the window seems to help. The smell of coffee has an opinion, and while walking to get another cup an old teacher is heard from in memory. Books call out from the shelf, offering references and distractions like Sirens tempting a sailor. Still the word will not come. Moving ahead the writer still can't let go of the search. Distractions abound. Yet another misspelling is stumbled over and the dictionary is pulled again from its rest. After looking up the correct spelling, the writer's eyes inadvertently slide across the page only to find the right word sought earlier with no avail. A small laugh is heard. Work continues.

Talents reveal themselves throughout a thing's life. One child is a prodigy at six but spent by twenty; another person doesn't do much as a child but blossoms after forty. Some talents we don't find until old age, and some talents don't show up until we are dead and remembered. Many times talents show up during periods when a person steps out of the normal flow of things—a convalescence or an extended trip, for example. Perhaps at such times interest is freed from habit and allowed to follow its own head. The important thing for style is that talent be tended all along in whatever form it takes. I might have a gift for gab, for example, a talent that has taken many forms over time—bartender, student, lawyer, lecturer, charter captain, and writer. The list could go on and on, and in addition to these occupational forms there are the countless other ways that this talent with words and language might play out in my interactions with the other things of the world. But in whatever form it takes, talent always wants to be accomplished with style.

Talent and style educate one another and in so doing lead us into the potentials they offer the many things of the world. Words might pervade a writer's imagination, say, while sounds fill the musician and the mathematician is beset by the feel of numbers. Living a life in the context of words is different than living one in the context of music. Thinking itself occurs differently in imaginations educated and trained by different talents. The writer hears words and so is influenced by their range and structures; the musician hears tones and melodies and is influenced by their range and structures. Each are exciting and pleasing ways of experiencing the world, each is as good as any other, each reveals the other things of the world in its own way, and each offers its own special opportunity for talent and its progeny. In each case style is expressed through talent at the same time talent educates and influences the expression of style.

As we will see more fully in the next chapter, talent is discovered and nurtured through contact with the other things of the world. Tools, especially, evoke and educate talent. Musical talent might possess a boy but he will not be a pianist until he finds a piano. Talent involves us in intimate, sensual contacts. Some things work and some do not. It is a piano and not a violin, sewing and not goldsmithing. Something special reaches out to us and suddenly talent arcs across this intimate space, sparking new possibilities. A skilled mechanic of seventy remembers the first time he heard the sound of an engine as a boy, how he was drawn to this sound and knew he had to know all about it. He speaks lovingly of dual carburetors, the smell of oil and gasoline, the murmur of the garage hands at work, and of old cars now gone that are missed like lost friends.

Talent learns most of what it knows from the things it works with. Ultimately it is the engine that teaches mechanics, the guitar that teaches proper fingering. From the perspective of style, then, the main thing is to honor the talents we are given through practice. This is accomplished through doing, which is what talent wants to begin with. People of exceptional talent almost always say that practice is what they love most. For them, performance is just practice with people watching. Talent shows up first in small things and continues to be nurtured even at its highest levels through small refinements. For some mysterious reason the child is drawn back to the piano and cannot stop fingering its keys. A simple scale is learned and this learning delights and encourages the child. Next a song is engaged. For weeks a particular measure eludes the young hands. But then one morning the hands break through and the measure joins its friends in song. The child rejoices and at the same time is encouraged to go on to the next song, this one a little more difficult. Step by step and inch by inch a promising talent is thanked and honored through practice.

Talent often is revealed by those things that encourage us to the challenges and pleasures of practice. What a thing is drawn to and challenged by is very important both for talent and for style. In the lives of exceptionally gifted people it is rarely the ideal of great success and fame that drives them in pursuit of their talent. Instead there is a kind of ethic derived from the work talent requires, a discipline that demands and delights in practice. Talent is more satisfied with a well-played piece in the practice room than with a lesser playing before a throng of admirers. Grand goals don't seem to do much for talent. But watching the hands do something that they couldn't do before—those are the moments that matter most to talent.

Talent, then, is not a passive matter but calls upon things to respond responsibly to what they have been given. This pressure to do right by the talent one has received seems given with talent itself. Talent wants to be practiced, wants to show what it can do, and so we strive to live up to our talent and its expectations. Talent delights in doing, but it can grow anxious, and worse, when its demands are neglected or ignored. Few things place us in more peril than failure to heed a godly call.

In many ways, talent is where style learns the most about responsibility and discipline. Great talent requires great discipline, and great discipline ultimately depends on devotion. Only the disciple, the learner, has a chance to receive the secrets that talent offers. As talent pulls us more and more into its capabilities we learn from its practice about what is possible. There is something in talent that holds each thing in this way, concentrating its mind and actions, compelling its return even when it becomes tired and frustrated. Something in talent makes us keep going back, returning to respect and answer the work to which we have been consigned. And, when we have done the best we can do, there is a feeling of pleasure combined with bittersweet imperfection. The painter looks at the finished canvas and sighs. The practice of talent, like all devotions, brings the feeling of the possible just beyond our reach. One more step, one more inch. The styles of all things are so moved by talent. Each thing striving to do what it does best, to serve well, to make a good showing. All things know both the pleasure and the whip of talent.

Just as all things share the responsibility of being responsible to their talents, they also have expectations about the talents of others. Certainly the other things of the world see our talents as well as we do, sometimes better. Indeed in most cases of exceptional talent there is someone who perceives and encourages such talent in its infancy. And so talent says that we must carefully heed the other things of the world if we are to be alert to their, and our, talents. We must pay attention to what the other things in the world depend on in us, what they seek us out to do. They depend on our talents just as we depend on theirs, after all, and sometimes everything needs a little prodding. The expectations that other things have of us are not necessarily borne out of pride or control, which would replace the selfless with selfishness. They are simply expectant, waiting for us to do what we can do, excited about the prospects of what might happen next. Everyone loves a good show, and in the world of style everything has something good to show.

And so perhaps we are back to that earliest meaning of talent as a measurement of weight, especially one associated with monetary value. Perhaps talent is how we measure our actions against the weight of potentials given to us and to the other things of the world. Perhaps talents are how the things of the world take each other's measure, seeing what each thing is made of, testing its mettle, weighing its worth. Perhaps talent is a currency between things, a medium of exchange and barter where each thing gets to display its wares while inspecting those of others, all things waiting to see what the market will bear.

In the end one thing seems sure. Each thing has been given at least one talent granted to no other thing—the opportunity to practice one's given gifts with one's given style. No other thing has ever been given this precise opportunity, and no thing ever will be again. No other thing can go to the keyboard and pick out the song that you have been sent. Not even the gods can be other than they are. But if each thing hears its own call, then this is a common calling that is shared by all things and we might learn to delight in our appointed tasks. Talent is a compelling force, tugging each thing back to its designated style and declaring a shared responsibility in all things to do right by the gifts we have received.

Amen.

CHAPTER EIGHT

Tools

We return now to a theme sounded in the last chapter but put off until now because of its special significance for style. Tools are essential to style. In many ways tools and talents are inseparable, you simply cannot have one without the other. But tools figure in all aspects of style. They are the necessary helpmates to style, but they also are presences in their own right. Without tools nothing gets done, nothing gets made. Even toolmaking itself proceeds according to the logic of tools.

Along with language, it is often said that toolmaking and the use of tools is what set our early human ancestors apart from other animals. Although other animals use tools, human tool use according to this view is qualitatively different, elevating the human to separate status. The general idea seems to be that as human intelligence grew our cleverness with tools grew, too.

But there are other angles on this story. Some researchers suggest theories more in keeping with what we have been saying about style. The hand itself, they argue, and by extension the entire body, is an active, necessary part of intelligence. The hand teaches the brain as surely as the brain teaches the hand. The hand, in turn, could not do what it does without the arm and shoulder, which also contribute to learning, and so on.

This intriguing idea brings with it another one. The manufacture of tools may be the genesis for spoken language and our social sense. There is archeological evidence that many of the tools used by earlier humans required more than one person to make. Imagine. As one pair of hands steadied the large rock, another pair hammered away, shaping and sharpening. Over time the rocks teach the people how to do this shaping and sharpening, and how if the rocks are held one way it doesn't work but if held another way it does. The rocks themselves teach which ones are best for which tools. Rocks like those over there are known to splinter when struck, leaving pieces useful for some tasks but not the ones sought after here. For this particular tool other rocks are needed. The people learn from each other, too, working together, gesturing and grunting as to how the rocks should be held, and as they do so their facility with gestures and grunts are refined over time by the work and tools at hand.

One person is known by the others to be best at shaping and sharpening. Another person has strong hands and so is relied upon to hold the work steady. Still another person is best at selecting the rocks to be used for a given task. And yet another is known to be good at coordinating things and keeping fights to a minimum. Tools evoke these talents, each person showing to the other people how he or she can best serve. According to such a scenario, tools are not the product of civilization but rather the other way around. At the very least, tools, language, and civilization arise together.

From the above we can readily see the necessary connections between tools and talent. Tools enable talent at the same time talent puts tools to their best use. Indeed talent has the power to teach tools about themselves, showing them capabilities heretofore unknown even to the tool itself. Facility with certain tools is itself an indication of talent, a much needed ability that can be read and appreciated by the other things of the world.

The view that we are taught by tools is squarely in line with style's interest and confidence in the many things of the world, and challenges other views that would emphasize the centralized location of intelligence within the skull and brain of the individual human. As with temperament and talent, tools, too, are here threatened with their own version of internalization that would remove them from their integral place in the world of things and reduce them to mere results of a self-improving brain. Only now are researchers beginning to realize the distortions imposed by such a brain-centered view. Style sets aside this internalized view, emphasizing instead that tools have their own power to teach things about what is possible in the world.

Tools are wonderful teachers of style because they teach us that to learn about a thing we must see it for what it is in its own context. Tools connect to certain things and not to others, and are more useful in some applications than in others. We learn about tools from using tools, each tool teaching us about its particular use and, by extension, about usefulness in general. If someone hands us a tool unknown to us, we can ask what it is and learn a name. We can ask what it does and what it is for. But only when we begin to use it does the tool's design and shape begin to take form. The tool helps us to imagine how it works, seeing how it turns the earth or affixes a button. Style extends this lesson to our interaction with all things, urging us to learn about things by watching what they do and following their lead. Style says that it is not fair to criticize the anvil for not floating. Each tool has its place and through this very fact teaches about the necessity of context.

To teach us about themselves tools must also teach us about the things they are designed to serve. Nothing exists in isolation, and so tools place us in a particular context among particular things. They teach us about the natures of things and how various things respond to one another's presence. A knife teaches about cutting and slicing and the possibilities of sharpness. Tomatoes respond to the knife's use in one way, bone and gristle another. Through these various interactions we learn about the qualities of those involved. We might even imagine that tools take delight in learning about the other things of the world as they are used in connection with them. The screw snug in its hole, the latch secure in its fastening.

A wrench will teach an observant user how to use a wrench. Its shape and design will suggest its purpose and through practice the hand will learn how to hold and maneuver the wrench to best advantage in different applications. But the wrench also teaches about the nature of nuts and bolts, the suitability of joining certain things together in certain ways, the advantages and mathematics of leverage, the limitations of space, and the importance of proper dimensions that suit hand and job. A stripped head teaches about the nature of tolerance and the relative hardness of different metals. A sheared bolt teaches about torque, stress, and the weak points in things otherwise strong. Skinned knuckles teach about what happens when you move too fast in the wrench's world, or over-reach, or start too soon, or press too hard. Much finesse is required in tightening and loosening. The wrench lives in a hard world and can teach hard lessons but it also teaches that there are all kinds of hard. Hard is full of grades and combinations, hard in some ways and not in others, each hardness having its own peculiar strengths and soft spots.

The making of tools teaches about the possibilities of making. The word tool itself originally meant to prepare or dress some raw material for further use or manipulation. In particular it referred to preparing leather, and is thought to come from roots meaning to flog or thrash. This active sense of tool as something things do to other things is still in the word, as when we speak of tooling leather to engrave it, or tool a book's cover to impress it with a design.

Imagine how long it took our pre-historic ancestors to learn how to prepare animal skins for use. They had no how-to manual to follow, and no teachers to turn to except the materials given them. Think of all the trials, all the errors. The learning and teaching was going every which way — the animal skins calling for and responding to certain tools — the people striving to make tools to achieve the results they imagined — the tools teaching about the durability and weaknesses of the skins. Under the influence of tools everything happens at once, all things teaching each other and learning from each others as their tools guide them into the possibilities of making. And in the process they find that they can create something that has never been before.

Tools seem to favor mistakes as much as successes, seeing both as useful in their own ways. We recall Socrates and the voice that guided him by saying no. Another great maker and user of tools, Thomas Edison, proudly said that his early experiments on the light bulb were not failures because he had in fact found 10,000 things that didn't work. Style shares this view that it is as important to know what doesn't work and what won't fit as it is to know what is effective and fitting. As much is learned from mistakes as successes, and tools are excellent at teaching both. Use the wrong tool to hit a nail you're holding and you will quickly learn why it is the wrong tool.

All things are tools for some other things. Toolmaking does not belong only to the world of the hard. Ideas are tools. Songs are tools. The other things of the world are tools. You and I are tools. Everything is used by some other thing to make things possible that would not otherwise be possible. All things are raw materials to some other things. All things are worked and shaped by other things to create new toolings and impressions. We might say that we do not like to be used, but it is the nature of things both to use and be used. Being used is a sign that we are needed and effective, and may indicate some special context where we are especially useful.

That each thing is useful to other things, and especially so to some things in particular, reveals aspects of the thing's style. Style shows, and other things perceive, how things are useful, where and how they fit, and how they can best be handled. Style also is revealed when something is found to be the wrong tool for the job. And when we look at something as a tool it begins to show us aspects of itself previously unseen and unappreciated.

As the wrench teaches us about the materials on which it works so all things have something to say about things on which they work. This is true the other way as well, the bolt also teaching us about the wrench. This is a wonderful idea for style, that by watching and learning from things in their given context we increasingly see the necessity for things. Wrench and bolt were made for each other, not only in the forge but also in terms of affinity and affection. It sometimes seems that there is no tool that does not eventually require broad and sophisticated learning for its proper use. So much is implicated in the act of doing. The high school student hates math but spends hours playing guitar. As talent progresses and the guitar requires more and more from the student he begins to be fascinated by alternative tunings and the possibilities of musical forms. Counting re-enters the student's life but now is welcomed as a necessary tool. Harmony teaches proportion, fractions are lived in three-quarter time.

Tools also influence style by teaching the pleasures and possibilities of manipulation and talented handling. There are few pleasures as rewarding as being well-handled with talent, respect, and even love. Talent loves few things more devoutly than the tools which favor it. A football player sits down on the sideline, tired and winded after a long game. A stray football lies by his feet. Within seconds the ball is in his hands, spinning and tossing, two hands playing catch with one another. The player just cannot leave the ball alone, he wants to hold it, play with it. This is the way of things and their chosen tools; there is so much affection, so much love. People cry over lost wrenches and broken shovels, reminisce over discontinued paints, grow angry when trusted tools are mistreated, and want, really want, that new lawn mower at the hardware store.

Tools and manipulation go together and can teach things about abilities they didn't know they possessed. Things flourish through manipulation, are capable of magic. The cards fan so flawlessly, seeming to pull the fingers along in their rush to be offered and picked. The coins flash and disappear, delighting in their amazement. Style shines through in these small flourishes and little tricks. The cards and coins give the hands so much, and with these tools in hand the impossible is made to happen before our very eyes.

Along with manipulation, tools teach style the ingenuities of improvisation. That tools can be adapted and combined in ingenious fashions shows that not even tools know all of their capabilities. Challenges create the opportunity, and sometimes the dire need, to use what is at hand, to see in things possibilities not normally seen.

But even as we use a tool do a job it was not intended for, we reiterate the proper place of things. A jury-rigged repair can show great improvisation and resource, but it will never be as good as the real thing. Tools admit to great flexibility, and will serve in many different situations if called upon in a pinch, but they nevertheless have their chosen ground. Tools strain when used in applications that call for other tools.

This is a useful lesson for style. Style wants to show itself in its own way in its own context. Of course things can be called upon to do things for which they are not suited. Of course we can twist style to fit an emergency situation. But such situations can place unusual burdens on style, bringing to bear forces for which it is not designed or prepared. It is better to let the style of each thing do its work in the place it belongs. Perhaps this is why talent so often emerges when people are in situations that take them out of the normal course of things. Perhaps this time out allows them to see that their talents were not being used to their best ability or that they were applying themselves in the wrong areas. Perhaps the stresses of using, or being, the wrong tool for the job are what required the time out to begin with. People who love what they do often talk in terms of finding the right fit or niche for themselves. Could this feeling of pleasure and confidence be the way a tool feels when it knows it is the right tool for the job?

Tools often show us that design is more important than force. Indeed forcing things is probably the biggest mistake one can make with tools. A small change in angle or a better tempering of steel can make all the difference between a tool that works well and one that does not. Tools seem to encourage us to make them better. The more we work with tools the more we move toward their fulfillment. We sketch and draw, filling notebooks with variations on the tool's theme, seeing something perfect in them.

And finally there is the sheer beauty of well-made and well-maintained tools. So much effort is made to ornament and personalize tools—from intricate inlays of pearl and gold to a name etched into a well-worn handle as a sign of belonging. Some of the earliest tools made were used for drawing, painting, jewelry making, and other delicate creations. Tools and beauty seem to go together, each appearing and furthering the other's cause. Even Greek myth suggests this affinity, marrying together Hephaistos, the toolmaker for the gods, and Aphrodite, the goddess of beauty.

Style is both given and made. What is given is not of our doing; our temperaments, tastes, and talents are gifts from beyond the pale of our comprehension. But we do have a hand in the making. Tools give us this opportunity, opening the doors of imagination to the possibilities of things not yet made. Better tools, better processes, better materials—always we are given the chance to make things more beautiful, to design a better mouse trap. Without tools we would have only time on our hands; with tools we are given an opportunity to bejewel the ordinary.

It is too often said that tools set us apart from the other animals. Style has a different view. Tools don't set us apart from the other things of the world but rather increase our responsibility to them. The other things of the world see and respect our use of tools. They know what we can do. And they also have great insights into how these gifts might best be used. They watch expectantly, depending upon us to do right by our talents and to take care with our tools.

As a young boy Pablo Blasco, who would later take his mother's maiden name because he thought it more distinctive, had a difficult time in school. Teachers struggled to teach the boy to read and write, and he applied himself best he could, concentrating to the point of sometimes getting lost in his concentration. Tutors were hired to teach the boy mathematics but this, too, seemed impossible.

Efforts to teach young Pablo seemed to wash over the boy. He was neither willfully disobedient nor by any indication lacking in intelligence. Indeed later in his young life, when he was called upon to pass entrance examinations to a desired school, he did in a day what others took weeks to do. He was not, as we might now say, learning impaired.

Throughout this time in his life all young Pablo wanted to do was paint. He was happiest with his easel set up beside his father's in his father's studio. And throughout this time everywhere young Pablo went, even when far away from his easels, he carried with him his trusty paintbrush. He always had that brush with him, close at hand. Faithful tool. Picasso's friend. Maker of destiny.

CHAPTER NINE

Teachers

Teachers educate us in many ways, but perhaps the best is through their open-hearted willingness to show us their own styles unblemished by pretension or affectation. Through their selfless display they lead us out of ourselves, releasing us into a waiting world having learned the courage of forbearance and a sense of the common. All things have the potential to teach us in this manner, but in this chapter we will pay special attention to those things that actually set out to encourage learning in others and whose intent it is to enable other things to more fully engage their styles.

There are all kinds of teachers who teach all kinds of things. One teacher might be especially adept at educating things to engage their temperaments. Another is a teacher of taste, helping things to refine and expand their preferences. And of course there are teachers of talents and tools who assist things in following the lead of their given abilities. The best teachers, as we shall see, keep all of these essentials together, knowing that what is essential is always there and so cannot be left out or ignored. Indeed one of the greatest things a teacher can do for a student is teach him or her to live within the context of the student's particular gifts, working with what one has been given and making the most of the unique opportunities bestowed by style.

One of the teacher's special talents is the ability to see talent in others. In the lives of almost all people of exceptional talent there have been teachers who appeared along the way to hold up a mirror to their talents. Many times, teachers are the first to see the glimmer of talent in the rough. What others might see as willful disobedience or lack of attention, the teacher sees as reactions to undue restrictions and boredom. What others might see as quirky nonconformity, the teacher sees as righteous rebellion in the face of settled determinations about how things should be. It may even be true that every student must await the right teacher, such precise guidance being necessary to talent's trajectory. Similarly, teachers depend on the talents of their students to keep them going, to challenge the set and known by asking direct questions with impertinent insistence. Students constantly remind teachers that one is never really done learning the basics.

Over time, each thing finds that it can learn from some teachers and not from others. Here again we see style revealed through interest and affinity. Sometimes teachers even get blamed for killing an interest in a student, a bad math teacher turning a student against math forever, and so on. But such stories beg too many questions. There are too many stories of other students persevering in their interests and affinities despite (because of?) obstacles thrown in their way by poor teachers.

It is an indication of style that certain teachers and students are drawn to one another. Teachers and students provide the necessary mutual context and containment for learning, and together reinforce style's lesson that it matters what comes together with what. From the self-correcting perspective of hindsight, it often seems as if certain teachers and students, like certain hands and tools, were made for one another, one teacher finding it difficult to maintain patience and interest with a particular student while being able to give all to another student. It is a basic lesson of style that one size does not, will not, and cannot fit everything.

The unique connection between one teacher and one student shows up again and again in the biographies of exceptionally talented people. Against the powerful foreground of this connection, other aspects of learning fade into a dissonant background. Over and over again we hear people of exceptional talent complain about school being too generalized and mass-produced. They are especially harsh about the tendencies of schooling to enforce the status quo. Stay in your seat, says this perspective, keep quiet, follow the rules because I said so, you're not ready for that project because the rest of the class isn't ready for such work yet, why can't you just be quiet and do your work like everyone else …. Such restrictions chafe talent, fraying it through demands for mediocrity and sameness—standardized tests, we call them. But standardized for whom?

On the other hand, many of these same talented people point with affection and admiration to one or a few special encounters with particular teachers. Tutors and mentors seem especially important for these people, as if the relatively narrow task of living into one's temperaments, tastes, and talents requires similarly focused guidance and encouragement. The student is called by invisible mysteries that are not so invisible to the teacher accustomed to looking for invisibles. The best teaching often occurs precisely when a teacher encourages a student to make his or her own way through the dark with hands outstretched, taking tentative steps into unseen terrain, senses alert for the next clue of direction, the next cool breeze that will say turn left, not right. Teachers cannot ameliorate the fear that accompanies such outings, but their sheer presence can show students that similar explorations have been undertaken before and are underway now by others who test the darkness with outstretched hands.

One of the teacher's great challenges is how to accomplish this highly particularized effort while also educating students to the many things that might be learned. Here are the students, fresh and green and new. How to encourage them to engage the many things of the world? How overwhelming learning can be! There is so much in the world, so many places where the students might go, so many places they might call home. Teachers must be willing to spread a bounty of possibilities before their students while knowing that out of this bounty only a few things likely will be desired. Out of all that is placed before a given student, he or she might prefer only one thing—no math, reading, or writing for me, thank you, but I would like to keep this paintbrush. Teachers must be optimists despite a steady diet of disappointment, like a chef who never tires of giving his guests something new to try.

From the perspective of style, we weaken teachers when we mistake their primary responsibilities. Too often we hear warm and fuzzy stories about a teacher who takes a student under wing, smoothing the student's way, stroking the student's self-esteem, urging the student on to greatness through praise and support, satisfied to have played some small part in the student's destiny. Here the teacher is seen as friend, surrogate parent, and kindly protector. Instead of leading the student beyond his or her self-interest, the teacher so envisioned is expected to serve the student by doting on the student's needs and feelings. Through a kind of role reversal the student becomes the guide with the teacher expected to keep pace, running alongside shouting breathless cheers and giving a thumb always up.

Here again we see the ugly, rearing head of internalization. As we have seen with temperament, taste, and talent, internalization dislodges teachers from their active role among the things of the world and so negates style. Once it is assumed that the teacher's primary responsibility is to the student's self-interest and feelings, the teacher is lost to the sucking vacuum of introspection. What matters to this romanticized view of teaching is how the student feels about the teacher, whether the teacher is liked or disliked, nice person or ogre. Teachers become judged by general election, praised for being popular or condemned for being insufficiently interested in the student as a person. The result is that all hope of learning is lost as teachers succumb to a gratuitous search for acceptance and approval.

Style sees things differently. We have said that to have style one must learn to see with style. If so, then a teacher's responsibility is to the style he or she sees in his or her students and not to the students' thoughts about themselves. Isn't this how the teachers who really touch us accomplish their magic, by showing us things about ourselves that we are unable to see? The extraordinary demands of talent, and the overwhelming nature of learning one's place in the world, are enough to make any fledgling run for cover. But what are we to do? Encourage such an avoidance of worldly responsibility in the name of self-appeasement? No, what matters most is not what the student wants but what wants the student, and so it is the teacher's obligation to pull the student from the briars of self-interest and to set them squarely before the powers that beckon. Rather than placating ignorance with platitudes of fear not, the teacher says hell yes there is much to fear, but quickly adds that hidden in such fear are unimagined treasures. It is not coincidence that treasures so often are sunken, hidden in caves, covered by debris and otherwise fraught with hazards to access and availability. Teachers encourage the hunt, promising only that when such treasure is uncovered it will reveal itself as such to an educated and appreciative eye.

Far more than being a cheerleader or confidant, the best teachers give students an indelible example of what it is like to live with certain temperaments, tastes, talents, and tools. What matters most is not the teacher's feeling about the student's self-esteem but rather the teacher's dedication to a field that might someday call to the student. Something about the student sparks recognition in the teacher, and in furtherance of this recognition the teacher seeks ways to excite and educate the student's temperaments, talents, and tastes. Various tools are displayed and offered to hand. What matters is not that teacher and student have an affinity for one another but that they share a devotion to a common affine. Student and teacher are on similar paths, but the teacher has had more time on the road. The student might even possess more talent than the teacher, but, if so, the teacher sees this as a positive development. Who would not welcome another pair of strong hands on the rope one is required by fate to pull?

Teachers can sometimes help students to bypass mistakes and detours by sharing the experiences they have learned along the way. But more than these helpful directions, and more even than the specialized information and knowledge that a teacher can provide, it is the example of the teacher that matters most. A teacher knows that students inevitably will make their own mistakes and encounter different circumstances than those made and faced by the teacher. And so the teacher serves the student by showing through example how to handle mistakes and missed turns. The student watches as a project on which the teacher has worked for three years suddenly fizzles out, or how an experiment designed by the teacher turns out to be based on an irreparably faulty premise. What does the teacher do in such cases? The student watches. The student learns.

Not all teachers meet their responsibilities with grace and courage. Some teachers teach by a negative road, showing through poor example how not to handle things. A crusty art teacher of meager talent berates a promising student because the student won't draw in a manner that suits the teacher. The student is forced to choose between compliance and failure and, being a promising student, chooses failure. Years later this same artist might speak of how this ugly encounter fanned her rebellious flames. In his own way, the art teacher unwittingly prepared the artist for her particular destiny as an artist, teaching her about the meanness of mediocrity and the obstacles of orthodoxy. Perhaps she will never forgive the teacher for his small mindedness, but she is nonetheless proud that she stood fast by her work. And, in moments of charity, perhaps she even thanks the teacher for helping to toughen her to the critics and naysayers that would always be part of her world.

The effects that things have on other things are always ambiguous and open to change. A teacher might think, for example, that he is doing right by staying on his students every second. One student remembers this attention as loving and supportive; another remembers it as pushy and controlling. And so from the perspective of style teachers probably do better not to worry too much about the so-called personal aspect of their relationships with their students. Teachers are meant to teach, after all, not to make friends or win popularity. It is curious that the teachers voted most popular by large numbers of students rarely figure in the lives of the greatly talented. Perhaps these teachers are simply too likable, too accessible, too pleasing to too many. Talent so often seems to prefer the fringes and the teachers who dwell there. Popularity matters little to style, which is more encouraged by watching and following actions tied to selfless service and dogged devotion. Years later a student might smile about the high jinks of a popular teacher, but it is the moody and depressive professor who didn't seem to like students all that much who is remembered as the real thing.

Teachers encourage style by encouraging showing. The etymology of the word "teach" itself means "to show how." We learn the styles of things by what they show us, and the more they show us the more intimate we become with their styles. Very often, what a thing shows us is dependent on what we are willing to see, our looking encouraging their showing. The best teachers teach us this, how to keep looking with honest anticipation as things change and refine before our eyes. Teachers of style emphasize both continuity and change, while also reminding us that we never can know for sure which is which. One thing might lead to another, but not even the gods know where things are being led.

The wonderful closeness that can develop between students and teachers has mostly to do with shoulder-to-shoulder work in a common field. Teachers see their students struggle with the work at hand and, where possible, help the students along. But teachers also know that struggle is part of the work, and so demonstrates through their own struggles how to proceed with grace. Sometimes students wonder why teachers won't step in more often to help. But over time students come to realize that their teachers, too, are struggling. As style more and more proclaims the student, he or she comes to realize that their expectations of help are impossible expectations, and with this realization teachers slowly are transformed into colleagues. A camaraderie of like spirits is formed. No longer is heard the narcissistic cry "help me." Instead, learned hands reach across generations to help one another in a common enterprise.

A teacher, then, can provide a glimpse into the future by presenting to a student a mature version of what is possible in the world that calls out to particular temperaments, tastes, and talents. Although the student's limited experience cannot yet fully appreciate the teacher's world, the style of the teacher, how he or she carries the responsibilities of his or her discipline, nevertheless makes an impression. Years later, a teacher's cryptic remarks or mysterious actions suddenly come into relief for the student. So this is what she meant, thinks the student, this is what she was trying to show me all along.

If the teacher teaches style by showing style, then the student learns style by observing style. Indeed the state of a student's learning can be seen in the quality of his or her observations about style. Somehow the two go together; style educating our abilities to observe while our abilities to observe educate style. The student encounters this lesson early on in attempts to imitate the teacher, whether the goal is to dice an onion or play a chord on the guitar. "Watch me," says the teacher, and so the student watches how the knife is angled and pulled just so or the fingers slide and pivot on the strings. Over and over the student watches, and over and over the student urges his or her hands to replicate the hands of the teacher.

Early attempts at such imitation can be frustrating, but the teacher can do little more than acknowledge the necessity of such frustration. Here again, the student learns to accept the slings and arrows of the work at hand by seeing how the teacher, wounds, scars, and all, persists. And so the student carefully watches the teacher at work, paying close attention to how he stands, how he holds the brush, how he stops to make tea or conversation, how he will not settle for just any blue but must mix and add and mix and add until just the right blue is achieved according to the needs of the image. Then, alone in the studio after hours, the student tries to stand as the teacher did and to hold the brush as he saw the teacher hold it. The student mixes and adds and mixes and adds, trying to see the blue as the teacher saw it, trying to understand what it was that told the teacher when to stop, when it was the right blue. The student mimics the teacher, hoping that somehow the teacher's gifts are contained in these actions and that, over time, the invisible impetus that guides the teacher's style might somehow breathe style into the student as well.

On its face such imitation is straightforward. Watch what I do and do the same. But eye and hand take a while to learn a new trick, and the first time things usually don't work so well. So you try it again. And again. This early and enduring emphasis on repetition suggests that it is a necessary aspect of imitation, a focal point of its practice. Moreover, this is repetition of a certain sort, repetition guided by something other than personal concerns or opinion. If it is a magic trick I am trying to learn, or how to tie a new knot, my personal feelings don't really matter all that much. The teacher's blessings and criticisms help me to shift my focus away from such personal concerns to ones that really matter, namely is it a trick that fools or a knot that holds. Imitation thereby disciplines students by connecting their styles to things beyond them, insisting that they put whatever talent possesses them in service to that which they seek to serve.

Discipline is a religious word. In its oldest form it means to learn, and a disciple is simply that, a learner. The best teachers are those who remain students until the end, their desire for learning burning hot as young love well into their ember years. As Socrates said, there is no learning without eros. Good teachers never forget that they are themselves disciples, learners called to teaching by the necessities of style. It is through fidelity to the requirements of their discipline that teachers most surely show students what is expected and what might be attained.

As the student mimics the teacher's acts of devotion and discipline he or she begins to understand that the hours of practice, the doing and redoing of the same things over and over again, and the unrelenting demands and needs of one's style are part and parcel of style itself. Here is the teacher's ultimate gift—that all that can ever be asked of anything is that it do the best it can in service to the temperaments, tastes, and talents that its style comprises. Once this lesson is learned, gone is the anxiety of having to do everything, which no thing can do. Instead the call to be all that you can be is not sweeping but specific. Here, right here, is where you can be of help. Style teaches that all contributions are necessary and that no one knows which ones will endure or which ones might someday ignite further contributions by other workers in the field.

Teachers do their best by us when they teach us how to continue learning after they no longer are there to help. They show us how to rig our little boat and how to set the sails. And then they watch as we take to sea. They cannot go with us, and we cannot stay with them, but at night, far from shore and familiar landmarks, we hear their songs in the wind. We know that they, too, are out there somewhere on their own little boat. And so we take our sights and steer our course, comforted by their invisible company, humming a tune we once heard them hum when they didn't know we were listening.

CHAPTER TEN

Tradition

Our last essential of style is tradition. We have seen that style is inherently multiple, and one aspect of this multiplicity is how style combines the new and the ongoing. In even the youngest gesture there is an indication of habit and ancestry already instilled. Each thing is a tradition unto itself we might say, but only when we remember style's basic lesson that no thing exists in isolation. In even the newest thing there are influences of long-standing that glitter through the surface of things like gold dust. Tradition embraces this mystery, showing style in terms of conventions, habits, and things handed from one thing to the next. Tradition bridges the gaps of generations with that which is beyond time.

Style appears in many ways, but among the surest are the conventions and habits by which we come to recognize and appreciate things. Consider. Two friends are talking and one tells a funny story about a mutual acquaintance. The other friend laughs and says, "that's just like him." Or a mother looks up from her reading as her young son walks in the room and instantly knows something is wrong. Or a person tells you a story and there is something in the telling that makes you suspicious even though you can't really put your finger on what it is that gives you this feeling. Such experiences are so commonplace that we rarely examine them for their mystery. And yet in each case we see an example of style showing through tradition.

The style of each thing contains its own tradition at the same time it places the thing within the context of broader traditions. There is a coherence to style, a hanging together of characteristics and mannerisms that is more than happenstance and is in fact given with the thing's style. As the other things of the world come to know us they come to know our continuing image, a tradition that endures over time. And the more intimately they know us, the more attuned they become to the nuances of our tradition, coming to depend on our lasting impression. Of course we might change in some aspects over time, but to those things familiar with our tradition these changes are simply added to the mix.

In the world of style, imagination encompasses perception. The mother looking up from her reading likely cannot tell us exactly what she sees in her son that lets her know something is amiss. The two friends would have a difficult time explaining what they mean when they describe some act as being "just like" their mutual acquaintance. And in trying to explain your discomfort and suspicion over a story that just didn't sound right, you might resort to words such as hunches or intuition. The reason such experiences escape explanation is that they do not belong to the world of explanation. Style does not explain, it appreciates. So it makes more sense for style to see such acts in terms of aesthetic responses existing between the various parties involved. In each case a thing shows itself to other things and these other things see what they are shown.

The style of each thing comprises its presence, interests, responses, and affinities. Taken together these things help to produce what we recognize in a thing's style. We feel its presence, note its interests, watch how it responds in its own context, and learn from its affinities. All of these things happen all at once, the thing's style showing itself as a cohesive image through the binding force of tradition.

Style has much to do with the natural associations that constitute a thing, and with the extraordinary fact that each thing always presents itself in accord with itself. As we noted earlier, nothing a thing does can ever be out of style with itself although we may well have to expand and deepen our appreciation to see this happy accord.

Tradition, then, holds together the multiplicity of style. We touched earlier on this mysterious force that holds things together in our discussion of affinity. Tradition adds that affinities are not only found between us and the other things of the world, they are found within the different aspects of our own style. Our temperaments, tastes, and talents require one another, depend on one another, and cannot be separated or torn apart. The tools we choose and that choose us are not just any tools but rather the tools that fit, that go along, that contribute to all of the other aspects of our style. Tradition is in all of these things, such that our every act already is laced with memory, each thing fresh with imagination that adds past to present.

Tradition shows up in a thing's conventions, habits, and quirks of long standing. Convention is a nice word for style, evoking a meeting or gathering, an agreement or compact reached through mutual consent, and a practice established through use and custom. The word itself comes from roots meaning to come together, and so tradition presents our style to the other things of the world as a gathering together of agreeable powers acting in accord with their own customs. Tradition presents a thing in the context of its conventions, showing the world how the thing holds together in customary fashion. Even the most outlandish actions are conventional in those prone to outlandish actions. Tradition shows style at home with itself, comfortable in the company of its many guests.

Closely aligned with tradition as convention is tradition as habit. Habit comes from a word meaning "to have," and its early meanings primarily referred to dress or apparel, a meaning still seen when we speak of a monk's habit or the riding habit worn by an equestrian. Only later did habit take on its current meaning as a regular pattern of behavior or settled disposition.

Tradition shows style through the dress of its habits. Lord Chesterfield once said that "style is the dress of thoughts," but we have come to see that a more accurate rendering is that thoughts are the dress of style. And not only thoughts, but all of the various activities and habits of a thing provide the dress of its style. When the two friends say it was "just like him" they are referring to this aspect of style, that they can see him dressed in such a fashion, recognizable from a distance by the habits he wears. Tradition reveals much about style through habit and custom, through the things that we do without thinking about it, through the customs that come as naturally to us as breathing. Habits have us, so to speak, as anyone who has ever tried to change habits understands.

The other things of the world see the habits in our style, they know what has us, and they also know how little we can change. It is through this ongoing appreciation of our habits that other things come to appreciate and depend on us.

None of this means that style is static or predictable. There is a great difference between being predictable and being dependable. Prediction goes too far by reducing the actuality of a thing's presence to the trajectory of my thoughts about the thing. Prediction requires abstraction, guess work, variables hardened to consistency. But a thing's style is not grasped through abstractions but in the face-to-face encounters of the many things of the world. Your gut feeling that you are being lied to is based not on abstraction but on a deep and abiding trust in the ways of things. You have heard so many stories by so many people in so many different contexts. Your ear is attuned to the subtleties of speech, its rhythms and cadence, the way that words appear on a face or speak through the body's language. And you have some sense of how the other things of the world act in your presence. You depend on such things without thought or reflection, the way you step out of bed every morning without first having to appease anxieties over whether gravity still holds its own. If thought preceded action there would be only stillness among things. Tradition allows style to rest easy, trusting in the given integrity of the many things of the world.

In addition to cleaving a thing's style unto itself, tradition places each thing within a broader context of support and understanding. Here again is the power of affinity, teaching us through tradition that all things have a place among the other things of the world. Each of the essentials of style connects us to ancestral powers, temperament reflecting cosmic influences, taste drawing us to recurring pleasures, talent committing us to ongoing work, tools teaching old lessons, teachers speaking with the timeless voice of common devotion.

One of the nicest ways I have ever heard of describing the power of tradition to locate us within the scheme of things comes from the psychologist James Hillman, who speaks of people being on trees, and that each tree gathers together people held by common interests and abilities. Among the people on any given tree there is understanding and communication. But understanding and communication wane among people on different trees. And so, for example, I might be able to read, understand, and enjoy certain writers while other writers are simply beyond me, out of reach on another tree. Style reinforces this idea, making clear through the things that hold us that it is here we belong and not elsewhere.

A thing cannot change the tree it is on through sheer force of will. Style's simple message is that each thing is what it is and can be no other. To struggle to fit where one does not fit cramps style, force feeding it food it cannot digest and making demands on it that it cannot keep. Style teaches that all things are limited in their capacity to appreciate the world; not even the gods of old were able to change places. If we today are irritated by such limitations it is in part because we have fallen from our respective trees into a thicket of illusory promises offering limitless choices. But no one can have it all or do it all. I cannot be a concert pianist no matter how much I want to be and no matter how hard I try if I have not been graced with the essentials required by such a calling.

We often discover the traditions that hold us through such shortcomings. It helps style immensely to know what one cannot do despite our most heartfelt desires. This is the crucible of tradition, the natural paring away of excess so that the sculpture within the stone might be revealed. Tradition seems to provide us with precisely the follies and detours we require to live more fully into our style. There is something telling about how I struggle against all hope to become a pianist even though those around me can hear all too clearly the futility of my efforts. Our inabilities prepare us for what we can do and offer us guidance by granting us the humility and courage to say "I just can't do it."

As style shows each thing to the other things of the world it gravitates to tradition. Tradition is like gravity, a force that reaches up to pull us down to join this meeting of like minds. Teachers, especially, help us to find this landing place by embodying tradition in a particularly visible way. Through their dedication to their work we learn about the necessity of dedication, about how nothing gets done that is not an act of devotion to some other thing, the way a book seems to need a dedication to get it started as a way of acknowledging the powers without which the book could not proceed. A libation to the gods, we might imagine, the way ancient festivals so often started with a small toast to the invisibles that made the festival possible.

When things are young they often fight tradition, feeling its gravity as undue weight and its requirements as tethers to flight.

But the particular nature of this fight, the enemies we choose and that choose us, themselves implicate style. That we rebel against some things and not others suggests the direction of our passions. Sometimes, in fact, the things we fight most are the very things which we cannot let go. Tradition without question carries with it demands of duty, honor, and obedience. Such demands can be too much for as yet unformed talents, causing us to run from seemingly impossible expectations. But this running away is style, too, taking us far afield so that, perhaps, we might feel the pleasures of homecoming.

Tradition gets a bad name when it is confused with dogma and fundamentalism. These latter ideas have forgotten that there are many ways to serve the same god. Indeed we might imagine that dogma and fundamentalism are tradition's own special styles of internalization. Just as we have seen with the other essentials of style, internalization removes things from their place among the other things of the world. And so dogma and fundamentalism insist that we may not look anew at the old, finding there treasures yet untold. Dogma and fundamentalism stop tradition in its tracks by preventing further elaboration, missing the simple fact that the tracks themselves show that tradition must keep moving. Dogma and fundamentalism post signs that stop activity. Do not touch. Hands off. But tradition loves to be touched, it requires maintenance and the loving care of many hands, the way law wants to be taken into the hands of those it serves. Tradition withers without the caress of loving hands dedicated to its reformation. Tradition hates dogma and fundamentalism, hates the way they try to stop its disciples from learning old tricks in new ways.

Dogma and fundamentalism pretend to answers that settle things once and for all. Tradition knows better. Tradition never says that this is the way things are once and for all because it knows that there is no such thing as once and for all. Tradition gives lasting life to style at the same time that style gives lasting life to tradition, providing a place for the eternal to gather, disperse, and then re-gather in renewed configurations, like old friends returning to an old place. So much is the same, and yet the details have changed. The old hangout is just the same, we say, but the bittersweet truth is that jukebox doesn't play the old songs anymore. This is the way of tradition, acknowledging the past in the present without trying to keep us in the past. Perhaps this is what the old ones were trying to tell us about memory, how despite its feelings of being past that memory always is a present reality. Tradition does not confuse familiarity with the same-old, same-old. Nor does it allow us to believe that what once was no longer is—the songs might have changed, but the jukebox is still there and there's a box behind the bar full of old vinyl.

Tradition teaches style about the lasting power of love. It is love that brings us back to the old themes that play through our lives, themes that we play out in the variations of our style. The other things of the world hear these themes like a bass line beneath our melodies providing the signature sound they have come to appreciate in us. That sounds just like him, say the two friends about their acquaintance. Only a few notes heard and they can name that tune.

In the end, all style is traditional, songs handed down one to the next for so long that the original author has lost importance. It is the song we know. There is something so pleasing about recognizing an old song played in a new way. But our delight in this newness could not be as it is if we did not also remember the old refrains. There are few greater achievements for style than to serve its tradition so well that concerns over singular authorship eventually fade, the way a good band supersedes its members, producing a sound beyond solo talent. It's a tight band, we say, pointing to the seamless blending of the mutual contributions made by its members, members who could not sound this way with any other band.

Tradition provides style with its context and thereby teaches all things about the necessities of context. Nothing can be as it is without what has come before. This does not mean that things are the result of their past, but rather that all things are constantly making memories. The past is not dead, said Faulkner, it isn't even past. And so tradition only feels old because that is the nature of its contribution to the imagination of style. Plato remains contemporary for those who share his tree, a colleague who can be called upon for advice and support.

The fragments of antiquity are like messages found in a bottle on a twilight beach. We don't know, really, where they came from or how long they have been lying there in the sand. We only know that when we read them they sound somehow familiar. We hold them in our hands and look out to sea wondering who wrote these words and how they came to be here. Then we take out our pen, add a few lines, re-cork the genie, and toss the tumbled bottle back into the retreating tide. We sit and watch the little raft until we lose sight of it in the bluing expanse. Then we get up, brush the time from our hands, and move along.

PART III

Obstacles to Style

INTERNALIZATION

IDENTITY

INTERPRETATION

SUMMARIES AND SUGGESTIONS

CHAPTER ELEVEN

Internalization

Before we begin our summary of obstacles to style, a caveat is in order. We have said repeatedly in the preceding pages that nothing is ever out of style with itself. Style does not look elsewhere than to what it is shown, and for style everything is always already there. As Oscar Wilde once put it, only a superficial person has to look beneath the surface. So when we speak of obstacles to style we must keep in mind that these obstacles, too, are part and parcel of style's proclamations. Like ambition that both creates and destroys at once, the obstacles we review here are not separate from style but rather are possessed by their own temperaments, tastes, and talents. They have their own tools and teachers and traditions that seek to further their own peculiar destinies. This being said, though, we will see that they distort the ability of others to appreciate style, biting the very hand that feeds them. They are, in a word, pests. And yet style seems unable to do without them. Like ants at a picnic they are necessary nuisances that perhaps help us to enjoy the ant-free days even more.

We might imagine each thing of the world as a simultaneous presentation by style of all that the thing is. We might imagine one translucent layer upon another, all showing through in such a manner that talk of layers does little to assist our appreciation. Who is to say what is surface and what below? For style, it is all right there before our eyes. Try to peel the onion to find its core and you are left holding nothing. And so the old man is already there in the boy, and the boy is unable to be the boy he is without the old man who is already present. Ancestors? There. Progeny? There. The timeless influence of the timeless? Always there. In the world of style the past is taken as a current event and the future is yesterday's news.

So to speak of obstacles to style is problematic. Nothing prevents style from proclaiming us because style is simply how things appear as themselves. But the obstacles we will consider lessen our recognition and appreciation of style by diverting our gaze and coloring our views. They are like tinted (tainted?) glasses that change the way things look.

The obstacles we will consider share the common fate of fundamentalism. All are ideas that seek to fundamentally proscribe how we imagine the other things of the world. Up to now we have been imagining a cosmos alive with purpose and intent. The world of this book cannot be reduced beyond the many things that are, and no attempt has been made to establish a central unity or wholeness beyond or above the actual appearances of the many things of the world. But now we come to ideas that would negate this world through various mandates and subterfuges. The obstacles we consider are shape-shifters, massive ideas that permeate and alter our most basic perceptions and thoughts about things. From the perspective of style, they are catastrophic in their impact, leaving behind fallout that covers all things with a toxic dusting of sameness.

———

Our first obstacle is one we have had run-ins with before, "internalization." As noted previously, Internalization is a word given to us by Owen Barfield, who himself acknowledged it as a rather ungainly word. It refers to modes of thinking that introvert the many things of the world into objects pertaining ultimately to the human being and his or her self-concerns. As Barfield puts it, internalization "is the shifting of the center of gravity of consciousness from the cosmos around him into the personal human being himself."

The results of this shift in gravity, says Barfield, are two-fold. First, the impulses that influence human behavior and destiny are relocated to within the individual. Indeed the idea that there is an individual "into" which such things can be relocated belongs to the world-view of internalization. The individual so defined then becomes the central concern in all affairs and is taken to be the only animating force among all things. Second, the life and integrity once seen as immanent in the many things other than human beings, the things that internalization christens the "outside world," grow weaker with neglect. Where once the many things of the world were felt as having their own native intelligence, dreams, volitions, and necessary place, internalization allows for such things as existing only within the human being.

So, according to this view, if I see a tree that seems to me to exude power and majesty I know that these feelings are subjective to me and not inherent to the tree. They are projections from my inner being onto the screen of an outside object. Why? Because trees are not things capable of such qualities on their own terms. They are not powerful and they cannot be powerful. They are only trees and it is my attitude toward them that gives them a semblance of power within my mind. Similarly, the happiness I see in my dog when I return home from a trip is my own imagination, not an accurate description of something my dog is capable of experiencing on his own. He is only a dog. Internalization is revealed in this insidious and insulting "only."

Internalization collapses the many things of the world into a fragmented human community of individual consciousnesses, if community may properly be applied to such a collection of freestanding and essentially solitary individuals. The classic motto of this move comes from Descartes—"I think therefore I am," a rallying cry for the lonely in a world re-shaped by internalization.

Internalization ignores Descartes' already present presence as he sits at his table writing his plaintive prose. Internalization sets aside the presence of things and chooses instead to believe its own version of creation and being. Internalization both begins and ends with a particular kind of thinking that relies ultimately on self-awareness. Incredibly, internalization sets aside the fact that such self-awareness exists only in the context of the other many things of the world. Internalization seems unable to comprehend that it is only one presence and perspective among many, a telltale indication of fundamentalism at work.

Internalization poses two main problems for style. First, it distracts imagination by turning all thoughts inward through introspection. (Again we must keep in mind that it is internalization itself that postulates there is such an "inward" place to which introspection may so turn our thoughts.) Second, this penchant for introspection curtails interaction with the many things of the world as personal reflection takes the place of communal activity.

Internalization distracts imagination by personalizing all things. The wonderful mountains stretching across the horizon are beautiful because they seem so to you and me, not because they are beautiful in themselves. It is we who provide their beauty through our beholding eyes and appreciating minds. Without us they are nothing.

The idea of the self and its many hyphenated progeny belong to the tradition of internalization, and collectively serve as wayward stations of the mind, places where things go missing and are never heard from again. In the mind of the self, the things of the world matter only because they matter to us and so we become preoccupied with figuring out how they matter to us. But there is no figuring out that is sufficient to satisfy internalization's voracious appetite for figuring out; there is always more reflection called for, more examination needed, more tracing of this or that assumed result to more distant and certain causes.

Despite all of the effort required by such examinations, internalization entices us with the promise of self-knowledge and offers us a sweet place of comfort and security where we have set procedures to follow and known outcomes for which to hope. Given enough time and reflection, says internalization, orderliness is possible in all things. Given enough time and reflection, we can come to know who we are and what we are meant to do.

But the purported sweetness of this place cannot hide its poisonous effect on style. Style cannot bear to be left shuttered in a room alone, no matter how many games and diversions internalization provides for us there. Style longs for the other things of the world, to see and be seen. Style longs to meet the responsibilities and to engage the opportunities granted to it by the other things of the world. Where internalization insists that "the unexamined life is not worth living," style retorts that the unlived life surely is not worth examining.

Introspection is a favored helpmate of internalization and a pervasive habit of the modern mind. Introspection's natural move is to look inward, convinced by its own actions that the truth is not out there but in here, inside my brain and its mindfulness. Other things become imagined as outside or beyond an inner self available only to introspection. Only on the inside can we discover the true meaning of things. Surfaces are not to be trusted because we have discovered there are disguises in the world. Perceptions and hunches are suspect because we know that there are illusions and we remember past mistakes. Only through the incessant inward probing of introspection may we come to know things as they truly are. Introspection thus provides its own illusions of focus and clarity as it camouflages internalization's world-grabbing enterprise.

When we speak of the other things of the world in terms of their meaning for us instead of from their own point of view we act under sway of internalization and its world-killing perspective. And so we travel to a vacation spot to see a particular sight but are disappointed when it doesn't look like what the travel brochures promised. Postcard pictures become the standard by which we judge, and thereby taint, actual experience. We want a sunset on the bay and all we're getting is rain. Nature is not living up to our expectations. We are disappointed. Unseen is a small bird delighting in a fresh water shower. Here is internalization at work.

When we declare that soul and spirit belong only to the human, while all other things follow immutable laws of nature, we act under sway of internalization. Indeed the very idea that there are set laws governing the many things of the world belongs almost wholly to the tradition of internalization. The game is over once the decision is made that all things can be reduced to physical laws judged according to experimental and mathematical criteria. Such "explanations" (another idea belonging to internalization and meaning at its root to "flatten out") are then taken as the only "true" or "real" things that can be said about something. Causality reigns supreme and the great search for historical origins begins. Once engaged by any of these activities we are operating in the world of internalization and according to its mechanistic mannerisms and characteristics.

Internalization's attempt to regulate and control all things gives rise to a persistent anxiety. This anxiety seems to be given with internalization's presence. Feelings of insecurity rise exponentially the more it tries to impose its order on things. And yet no amount of force or control seems capable of eliminating the free-floating anxiety in which internalization lives. It is as if some part of internalization recognizes its own tentativeness despite its confident claims and imperialistic designs.

Along with introspection, internalization further distracts imagination by one of internalization's favorite games — the positing of opposites and the demand that we choose between them. This emphasis on opposition and choice, however, as if alternatives are actually present, cannot hide the singularity of internalization's game. Only internalization needs to set up such antagonisms, and they are legion — science against religion, mind against body, rich against poor, white against non-white, east against west. But dilemmas exist only when choices are constrained to two by a singular perspective. The lens through which internalization sees the world might have many angles, but it is a single lens. Choice between exclusive alternatives belongs to the style of internalization and not to the many things of the world.

We come now to internalization's second deadening effect on style. Once imagination is distracted from the other things of the world, effective action in that world ceases as interest wanes. When internalization takes control, a slow inward spiral begins, sucking all things into its unfillable void. Style constantly leads to the other things of the world, impressed by their integrity and significance, and forever interested in their activities. Internalization leads only to itself, and changes our manner of speaking, our rhetoric, so that we speak of all things in terms of introspection. Actions then give way to motives. Where biography and history once spoke in terms of plans made and actions taken, internalization harkens a New Age of autobiography, the self telling about itself, and history comes to be understood in terms of personalities and psychological inter-dynamics.

Under sway of internalization, everything begins to be inwardly related to the human being. Until the seventeenth century, for example, the words "depression" and "emotion" were used only in connection with material objects; they were not applied to human beings. Internalization changed all that, subsuming these words into the inner self. Similarly, it took internalization to make "stress," a term belonging to metallurgy and engineering, into a word appropriate for human application. But perhaps the most glaring of all such shifts in meaning occurs with the word "subjective," which originally meant "existing in itself" but by the end of the seventeenth century means "existing in human consciousness." Internalization thus takes all thoughts prisoner to human consciousness, a word that itself belongs to the tradition of internalization. Left behind is a world bereft of all significance save that which we bestow from within our own minds. Beauty becomes a mote in the eye of the beholder.

Internalization abstracts humans from their place among the other things of the world. The effects of this abstraction in terms of people are many, some of which have been suggested here. But what happens to the other things of the world? How does it feel to not be noticed, counted, or taken into account? What doesn't like a second look, a little respect? How does it feel to be taken for granted instead of received as a gift of good will and possible interest? What kinds of behaviors accompany such feelings? Internalization would call such concerns mere speculation or worse, but for style such concerns are critical. For style, there is nothing worse than not being noticed. In the world of style, to not be seen is a sleight of cosmic import. Style seeks to appreciate the other things of the world on appropriate terms of their own making, following their lead and accepting their peculiar sense of time. Internalization instead defines things in its own terms, taking the lead and insisting that we dance to its beat.

When faced with cold eyes that see them only as agents of brute force in need of control and regulation, the other things of the world beat a hasty retreat from internalization and its desiccating gaze. Perhaps this is the distance one actually feels in abstraction, not us pulling away from them but they from us, the world falling away at our feet, leaving us hanging, not flying. Nothing likes to be approached as if it is already fully understood, and one sad aspect of internalization is that its own expectations leave it alone in an increasingly small and ugly world. Just try to imagine what a world would be like built strictly according to one's own specifications, how dreadfully dull it would be, how much would be left out through ignorance and bliss. Internalization locks us within such a world and then tries to find things to amuse us there, trying its best to keep us happily distracted from the bar on the door.

Having said all of this, however, it is folly to imagine that internalization can be overcome, such a fight being precisely the kind of fight that internalization's bullying seeks to pick. Things cannot live in worlds other than the ones in which they live, and internalization is a dominant influence, if not the dominant influence, in the modern mind. The modern mind, after all, is a creation of the modern mind, and this mind cannot be other than it is or live in a world other than the one it has made for itself. Internalization is intrinsic to human consciousness, a not surprising fact given that internalization creates the idea of human consciousness. And so internalization is not a separate perspective but a perspective that exists within all modern perspectives. Internalization's fundamentalist and monistic character is revealed through its omnipresence. Under internalization's sway, every perspective displays a tendency that would take everything else only in terms given by the perspective itself. When anything purports to elevate itself to higher fundamental status, to proclaim the true and the right, or to settle the question once and for all, that is internalization speaking, drunk on its own liquor. Internalization closes the shop, eschewing the many possibilities given by unions of unlike minds.

There is no getting around internalization so long as we live in a world crafted by its assumptions. The great irony is that the very thing internalization allows us to see most clearly, once we recognize its presence, is the style of internalization. Obstacle or not, we risk much when we fail to acknowledge internalization's long tradition, a tradition as respectable as any other in its proffered sincerities. We might even grant that it has much to offer to the other things of the world, so long as it is not given its own head for too long. Style can assist us here by calling internalization back from its introspections, back to the window to check the weather, eye the grass, or spy on a neighbor. With time and patience we might even coax it to come out and play.

CHAPTER TWELVE

Identity

If internalization hinders style by turning imagination away from the things of the world, identity makes matters worse by insisting on the singularity and supremacy of definition. The demands of identity and definition work against style's natural preferences for multiplicity and the nuances of imagination. For style, all things are multiple in their constitution and no thing exists in isolation. Style thrives in thriving, and it enjoys the fecundity of the many things of the world as a source of constant wonder and enjoyment.

Style, for example, enjoys words, lots of them, and likes to experiment with many different ways of saying the same thing, thereby teaching that the thing we are saying is not the same after all. For style, ambiguity can offer a kind of precision that escapes identity's penchant for clear and distinct understanding. Style appreciates metaphors, and recognizes their ability to be a most accurate way of speaking. Style strives to see each thing with as many eyes as it takes to see, knowing all the while that there is always more there for another look.

Identity's preferences and inclinations are given with its presence. As a word, it comes to us from the worlds of mathematics and logic and so speaks in a rationalizing style. The etymology of identity means simply "the same" and its clearest expression in the seventeenth and eighteenth centuries was algebraic, $x = x$. An encyclopedia of philosophy, appropriately enough, summarizes identity's context by noting that, from its very beginning, identity was associated with two general themes, permanence and unity. And that's just the beginning:

> The problem of identity as permanence gave rise to the problem of change, whereas the problem of identity as unity gave rise to the problem of universals…. Each of these problems, in subsequent generations, splintered into a host of related issues, some of them persisting to our own time. The problem of change, for example, gave rise to the problem of substance, problems about the relation between what seems to be so and what is so (appearance and reality), and the problem of personal identity; and the problem of universals gave rise to the problem of individuation and the problem of abstract ideas. (*The Encyclopedia of Philosophy*, Vol. 4, p. 121.)

Of special interest in this passage is that identity begins as "a problem" and then proceeds to spawn more problems. Identity appears in the context of the problematic and encourages the creation of problems and the work of solving them. Identity replaces mysteries with puzzles, and favors solutions over the pleasures of being mystified.

Problems of identity, then, which are ubiquitous in our times, are not surprising but self-generating. Identity and problems go together, making one wonder whether if when one appears the other can be far behind. And so when something becomes a problem, we might look closer to see if identity and its related issues are somehow involved. Certainly problems seem often to come down to questions of definition and identification. Does this mean that identity gives rise to the great tradition of figuring things out? Does identity arise from philosophy or is it the other way around? These are the kinds of questions that occupy the mind of identity.

There are many dangers for style in identity's didactic world. Especially troubling is identity's intolerant temperament. Identity is not content to co-exist with other perspectives but is pulled by its nature to replace various modes of appreciation with unified understanding. It cannot help but insist on the primacy of its interests and methods. Identity wants single and final solutions and is ready with another problem when we're done with the last one. Like all perspectives, identity is self-referential, but a distinguishing characteristic of identity is the singularity of its references, both in form and substance (to use two of identity's own distinctions). Identity is by nature exclusionary, believing that meaning, its Holy Grail, comes from definition and that definition comes from narrowing.

Closely related to identity's exclusionary tendency is its habit of speaking in terms of issues. Identity encounters the things of the world in terms of issues, demanding to know, before any further interactions can take place, what a thing is and what it wants. Identity, we might say, has an attitude. It is eager to stand its own ground even when no one else wants it, and if given long enough identity will find something offensive with which to take issue. Issue-oriented speech, then, especially when tinged with adversarial rhetoric, belongs to identity's self-defined world-view.

Our encyclopedia article goes on to say that identity "is a necessary though not a sufficient condition of someone's being accorded rights or being made to shoulder responsibilities." (Vol. 6, p. 96.) This suggests that identity prefers to relate to other things in terms of rights and responsibilities derived from identity's own definitions. Paradoxically this issue-based style of relating, although nominally designed to ensure good relations on well-defined terms, seems instead to raise constant problems by insisting on pre-established ground rules. It is not so much the ground rules that insult other things as it is identity's insistence that acceptance of the ground rules must come first. Demanding definitions and rules, after all, is already an act of defining and rulemaking, and thereby identity seeks to establish control over what is to follow. It's like asking someone to sign a prenuptial agreement on a first date. Only after identity has created properly defined individuals according to its own terms may such individuals be assigned rights and responsibilities, also defined by identity. Throughout, identity remains in control.

By contrast, style teaches us to avoid dealing with things in terms of issues and definitions and to focus instead on how things present themselves. Style helps us to learn how to be responsible to the other things of the world according to their customs instead of dictating to them what their responsibilities are according to our customs. For style, the things of the world do not present issues to be adjudged or rights and responsibilities to be settled but are taken as presences to be appreciated and respected.

We give voice to identity and its issues when we speak in terms of the changeless and the changing, the one and the many, of personal identity and the self, or of what is real and what is illusion. A comical aspect of identity's stronghold on modern imagination is that almost all efforts to speak against identity find themselves already using identity's terms. Diversity and multiculturalism, for example, with their heavy emphasis on personal definition and individual rights and responsibilities, remain firmly within identity's established clauses. Abstractions of race and gender and class belong to identity's mind. And protests against unity that, like this book, speak of "the many things of the world" also find themselves hopelessly trapped in identity's polarizing rhetoric. Like internalization, identity is one of the dominant perspectives of the modern age and there is little to be done except slowly to steer away from its edifying currents.

Style recognizes that identity's issues need not be accepted as applicable beyond the bounds of identity's own style. It is identity that uses words such as permanence, change, changeless, unity, one, many, diversity, race, gender, class, multicultural, self, ego, individual, rights, and responsibilities. Such words and ideas exist for identity, are real to its perspective, but need not be imported like kudzu to unsuspecting climes where they quickly begin to choke out the local flora. Style doesn't really need such words except when speaking to or of identity. Like all things, identity presents itself as itself ("itself" belonging already to identity), and so provides an atmosphere of certainty by its very presence. I am what I am, it says, and to its self-defining, *cogito* intoxicated mind what more can be said?

Even when identity speaks of the many, it does so by way of contrast with the one. Indeed it offers oneness as a promise to the many if only they will get their act together. And so there is little doubt about where identity's heart really lies. According to identity, if there appear to be many things we simply have not recognized that they are part of a larger whole. In the world of identity, the many exist only in the one, chaos is a failure to see or impose the unity inherent among all things, absolutes are real, churches become universal, and unified theories beckon science. Identity wins once we agree that things must be defined once and for all with mathematical certainty. Anything less means that more razor is needed to simplify things further. And so of course using more than one word for the same thing bothers identity because it already has decided that there is a "same thing" that should have only one closely defined meaning.

Style does not hold to such assumptions, and instead suggests that there are multiple perspectives on all things. Indeed even to speak of "things" implies more than we really know. Such designations belong to our minds and our language but are not necessarily appropriate elsewhere. Still, what is to be done? It is very difficult, if not impossible, not to speak through the rhetoric in which our age is immersed. But style reminds us to beware the limitations of our terminology and not to imbue identity's penchant for names and categories with metaphysical scope. This, from the perspective of style, is identity's great mistake and the heart of its fundamentalism— it believes in its own creations to the exclusion of all else.

Read five biographies of "the same" person and you will get five different stories. How can this be? Identity would chalk up these multiple perspectives to the separate personalities of the biographers, perhaps implying that they had their own issues to settle with the subject of the biography. But this only deepens the quicksand, begging the question of begging the question. Style, on the other hand, is not surprised that there are many stories to be told about pretty much anything. Style knows that nothing has enough eyes to see everything at once, and that this very limitation is what makes the world infinitely interesting to our finite abilities and that calls forth the necessity of community.

An old book, read a dozen times, continues to show new phrases as it is reread. Identity would say the book has stayed the same and that we have changed. The reason that certain phrases stand out now that did not stand out before is a function of our reading the book in the context of what is important to us now that was not important to us before. In other words, identity provides both its own underlying assumptions along with the rhetoric needed to discuss those assumptions. Style, on the other hand, wonders if the fact that a phrase stands out now that didn't stand out before might not be an act of prior restraint by the book in what it shows to whom and when. Perhaps the book knew we were not ready to really see certain passages; or perhaps it likes saving some of its pleasures for later enjoyment.

Identity finds such talk silly. Working in tandem with internalization, identity is transformed into personal identity and thereby lays claim to being the source of all feelings of animation in the greater world. Only we are animate. Only we have souls. Only we have identities. The inanimate are exactly that, "not-souled." Things have no identities save those bestowed by us. The traditions of internalization and identity do not, cannot, speak of animals, plants, books, or any non-human thing in terms of being or having a soul.

Identity precurses and makes possible the idea of the self. But self is not a useful idea for style. For one thing, the self is always "the" self, implying immediately a singularity or unity of perspective and concern. The ideas of self and its hyphenated progeny are regularly associated with ideas of wholeness and unity. The self urges us to pull ourselves together, to get our act together, to become one with the world (which is also imagined as a One), to get in touch with one's true identity, to individuate and thereby assimilate the many into the one, to work on ourselves (identity always presenting problems to be solved), and to become centered and settled of spirit. Self is interested only in self, and all things are taken only insofar as they have relevance to the self and its burgeoning, ever-becoming identity. Experiences matter because they matter to me, the sunset beautiful because it moves me to pleasure. How identity loves that word "because."

Even the anguish felt by the self takes the form of a selfish cry. A woman in therapy complains, "I don't know who I am. Who am I?" Such a question exists only for identity, which thrives on questions and problems of identity. But for style, the woman's complaint already tells much. Notice what the complaint sets aside. All of the things the woman demonstrably is and does are ignored in favor of an identity that can be arrived at only through introspection. What she is and does in her everyday life and activities, her complaint implies, are either lies or of no lasting significance. And so her complaining questions tell us how, if not who, she is with great specificity. We see that identity has stripped her of her worldly flesh to leave only an ephemeral inner self having no need for earthly coils. Her questions proclaim her a seeker of a truth that lies only within.

Once identity begins its endless search for the self it quickly encounters more than it bargained for. Instead of the unity and stability that identity would impose, it finds all sorts of ambiguities, mixed voices, divergent interests, and unaccountable oddness. And so it invents a range of ideas with which to mollify itself. Such things are not real, says identity, or at least not true. Identity defames the multiplicity of things as personas that disguise and mask our true inner selves. Unable to control the multiplicity that everywhere confronts it, identity simply defines away what doesn't fit, like old Ptolemy trying to make the planets spin according to the wrong plan.

Style reminds us that it is identity and its tradition that gives us notions such as levels or layers of consciousness. What identity does not or cannot recognize it labels as unconscious. What identity does not or cannot see it labels latent and hidden. And even what identity concedes as manifest it habitually distrusts. Identity is tightly wound and forever anxious, constantly trying to keep things together in a form that matches its expectations. Identity beats at the heart of paranoia.

If internalization separates humans from the other things of the world by abstracting humans from their place among things then identity tries to recapture this lost world with a net of definitions and unifying theories. But its goal ends ignobly. Once explained or defined we are done with things, identification putting an end to interest. The things of the world are pinned to a board, tagged and classified, the names given to them by identity identifying them once and for all as they squirm for a freedom that will be granted only by death. But the things of the world are not stupid, and it doesn't take long for them to recognize identity's net and what it portends. And so as identity approaches with its capturing intentions the many things of the world take flight, leaving identity and its issues in stumbling pursuit, cold in the growing alone. Perhaps this is why identity becomes so easily lost in self-absorption—everything else has taken off, leaving identity to its own devices, sadly deprived of what it needs most, the nearness and trust of the other things of the world.

CHAPTER THIRTEEN

Interpretation

Our third and last obstacle to style is interpretation; the practice of translating the unknown into the known. Like identity, interpretation hinders imagination by diverting attention away from the given mystery of a thing. Interpretation shifts all things onto its own ground and into areas where the interpreter is more comfortable and feels more knowing. Interpretation offers understanding and significance, but it does so in terms other than those provided by the things it encounters.

The problem with interpretation for style is encapsulated in the word "translate." Before it was applied to language, translate meant to relocate from one place to another. And so translation moves things to a different context, a different place. The results might seem more intelligible and known to the mind of the translator, but we are in a different place than where we were before.

Interpretation is something that is done to things, but it is not the same thing as that which it interprets. Interpretations are like the palimpsests of old, faded erasures over which interpretation illumines a new story. Interpretation might give us a new image in its own right, but this new image has only tenuous connections to the image that was left behind. A restoration of a faded fresco might be beautiful, but it is not the same thing as the original. Interpretation simply does not respond to things in kind; it does not speak back to things in the manner in which it is addressed. For its part, style does not insist on a common language shared by all but suggests that many languages are needed because there are many ways to say things. Unlike interpretation, style finds the things of the world infinitely more interesting in their own right than anything we might say about them.

Interpretation shares the views of internalization and identity that things are not as they appear. Interpretation, then, like internalization and identity, would have us seek the true significance behind the deceptive faces of things. Interpretation's fundamentalism is revealed in this paranoid predilection that insists something else is always behind what is going on. Interpretation insists that only it can provide the truth and meaning that things, left to themselves, are incapable of giving. Never mind that it is interpretation that demands things must have truth and meaning to begin with.

Style, on the other hand, is more curious than suspicious, and does not habitually speak in terms of truth or meaning. For style, whatever is, is. Note the difference between this formulation and Alexander Pope's claim in the eighteenth century that "whatever is, is right." This latter claim is a claim of interpretation, blending two strongly interpretative traditions, rationalism and Christianity in a moral proclamation of "rightness" that refers all things in their turn to Nature and Christ. But from the perspective of style, it is interpretation that adds this moralistic judgment to things. Style does not need such moralistic judgments and does not attempt to add them to what is. One has to wonder how interpretation can ever hope to do justice to things if it insists on replacing their laws with its own.

Interpretation begins with a necessarily limited and idiosyncratic base of knowledge and then tries to fit the unknown things of the world into this base, thereby taking an artificial structure as actual ground. And so, if I am a student of Greek myth then I will see mythical references in your life and dreams. If I am a follower of modern psychoanalysis then I will find untapped traumas in your mind and past. If I believe in the marketplace then economics becomes a holy exegesis with all things converted to their meanings for the ledger. Philosophers will of course insist that examination is necessary to life, their interpretations giving them exactly what they expect.

Interpretation, then, is that movement at work in all perspectives that seeks to translate things into one's own terms instead of remaining with the terms given by other things. Interpretation and fundamentalism share this relocating and bracketing tendency. Style would attempt to undo this relocation and bracketing of imagination by drawing our attention constantly back to the things of the world as they present themselves.

The formulation of interpretation as translating the unknown into the known sounds philosophical because interpretation is philosophical, a fundamental act of the mind conceived as mind. Style teaches that there is always a methodology already at work at the beginning of even the most self-effacing interpretations. Even professing ignorance and lack of wisdom gave Socrates a place to start. Given interpretation's innate bias, style cautions us against getting lost in interpretation's game. Beware the "Ah-ha!" that so pleases interpretation when it is able finally to make things fit into what it already thinks it knows. And beware especially when our interpretations ring with the sound of rightness.

In practice, interpretation lulls us by a retreat into the familiar. Where style remains ignorant and open before a woman who appears in my dreams, interpretation knows just what to do with her. Style doesn't know who she is or what she wants, if anything. Maybe she is just passing through. But interpretation knows. She is a representation of Athena, or a symbol for psychological conditions having their real significance elsewhere. To prove this fact we need only retire with interpretation to its waiting library, where we will find plenty of evidence to support it claims. Interpretation thus provides the comforts of signposts understood and directions followed.

Of special note, interpretation assumes that the woman in the dream has a meaning, a word not normally associated with style's effort to take things on their own terms. Style emphasizes that the things of the world are not subject to defined meanings because they are not in the first instance objects of or for my mind. Meaning is something demanded and provided by interpretation, and under the influence of internalization and identity these meanings almost always end up having human individuals as their final reference. Even if I interpret the woman in my dreams in terms of the gods, the ultimate question always seems to be what does this epiphany bode for me? We listen to a pianist play a classical tune and wonder what his phrasing says about his personality—this is interpretation's quick kill.

Back when the things of the world were considered alive with gods, interpretations were other than they are now. Then, interpretations were aimed primarily at divining prophecies and godly acts. Now, under sway of internalization, interpretation retains this old interest in prophecy but shifts the center of interpretive consciousness to the individual human. Where once the things of the world spoke with divine implications, interpretation now hears them primarily in terms of their ability to satisfy individual desires and meanings. Interpretations, not dreams, become wish fulfillments.

The assigning of meanings to things is in keeping with interpretation's preferences and inclinations. Interpretation deals in symbols instead of images, representations instead of presentations. The dove in this painting is the divine spirit, that snake in the grass the devil, that lion St. Mark. Your current insecurity points to something other than your insecurity, that is, your insecurity means something other than what it presents, it has a truer meaning and most likely a causal referent beyond itself. The plastic Mary on the dashboard is not sacred but rather represents and refers to the sacred; it is a symbol for the Virgin and not the Virgin herself. This is interpretation's basic assumption—that things are not as they appear and do not mean what they say. For interpretation, subterfuge and double-talk are everywhere the rule. And so of course it falls to interpretation to decipher an encrypted world.

By contrast, style is interested in symbols only to the degree that they are taken as things in themselves, including their referential natures. Style, in other words, does not look past a symbol for a hypothetical referent but instead keeps focused on the symbol and its symbolic ways, which is what style finds most interesting about symbols. But for style there is something undeniably sad about the dove that is left behind by our transcending interpretations. We might ask ourselves, who among us would want to be taken only as an example of something else?

Interpretation and its symbols capture time and action in frozen frames. The woman in the dream is doing all kind of things worth watching and talking about while interpretation focuses only on those aspects of her appearance that it can interpret, insisting on a script that it has already rehearsed instead of the improvisation called for by the moment. Style does not so press things to completion, and prefers that things take as long as they need to take to do whatever it is they are doing. So far as style is concerned, interpretations are shortcuts that too many people know about to places where too many people have already been. Style prefers the underbrush and the off-track. And style simply cannot comprehend, if it is this particular thing that we are curious about, why we would go elsewhere to engage that curiosity. It's like the old joke about the drunk who looks for his car keys under a street lamp instead of where he lost them because the lighting is better there.

Interpretations, then, are always purposive and are intended to meet certain predetermined theoretical and ideological expectations. Interpretations want something from the things on which they work, and generally appear to have a good idea of what that something is. Interpretation sees things as a maze is seen from above—it might take a while to figure out how to get to where we want to go but at least we know where that place is from the beginning. Every step of interpretation is charged with intent, purpose, and direction, and, once begun tends to run under its own head (witness how easy we get carried away with interpretations), driven by interpretation's own desires for self-fulfillment.

This last point is critical. Interpretation's self-actualizing qualities are of special interest to style. Interpretation's stubborn insistence on its own ways teaches very clearly that ideas are not passive, inert things but rather are forces with their own intentions and purposes. Interpretation wants to interpret; that is what interpretation does. And so we should not be surprised to find interpretation associated with all sorts of other ideas that further this desire. Meaning alone is a huge asset to interpretation; the more we are sold on meanings as the true value of things the more we will need interpretation to broker the deals. And although in our times interpretation usually endeavors to provide meanings of significance for human individuals, interpretation's primary interest is to keep on interpreting. Like other influential ideas, interpretation readily adopts the prevailing habits of the times to maintain its own viability and influence.

One of the great interpreters of our time, Sigmund Freud, gives us a good description of how interpretation looks at the other things of the world. His classic work, *The Interpretation of Dreams*, provides telling insights into the habits of interpretation, insights that for style say less about the interpretation of dreams and more about the dreams of interpretation. Why do we interpret in the first place? What does interpretation want? Freud is very clear on such matters.

For Freud, dreams are in particular need of interpretation. Why interpret? Because "dreams are disconnected," says Freud, "they accept the most violent contradictions without the least objection, they admit impossibilities, they disregard knowledge which carries great weight with us in the daytime, [and] they reveal us as ethical and moral imbeciles." (*IOD*, p. 87.) We interpret because dreams are "brief, meager and laconic," (*IOD*, p. 313) and are "more careless, more irrational, more forgetful and more incomplete than waking thought." (*IOD*, p. 545.)

Presented with a dream that is nonsensical, obscure, insignificant, disjunctive, and confused, interpretation is more than glad to provide meaning, insight, significance, context, and understanding. According to Freud, this is precisely what interpretation wants. Interpretation leads us "toward the light — towards elucidation and fuller understanding." (*IOD*, p. 549.) Little wonder that interpretation continues to build one interpretative layer on top of another, layers that interpretation then uses to justify the need for interpretative excavations. Interpretation provides "structure," says Freud, gives a sense of "higher unity," builds an "edifice," (*IOD*, p. 631) and erects "scaffolding" (*IOD*, p. 639) on which interpretation might base its understanding.

So far as style is concerned, it is bad enough that interpretation directs our attention away from things. But to make matters worse interpretation demeans the things it interprets in the process, as the above comments by Freud make painfully clear. Interpretation turns things into pale remnants of what were vital presences, creating representations from presentations, preferring ready references to ongoing research in the field, symbols to the enduring mystery and power of images. In each interpretative move we insult the things of the world by the clear implication that they could have done better. Our dreams are insufficient as presented and must be replaced with myths worthy of our self-value. Our foibles are not the petty necessities of life but the results of longstanding and hidden traumas now forgotten but still available to interpretation's omniscient memory. Once again the things of the world are lost, and what else can we do but take heel to follow the unraveling threads of our interpretations?

We might here remind ourselves about how we feel when we are the ones being interpreted. How does it feel to be interpreted, to have our words constantly taken as meaning other than what we say, our actions constantly seen as signifying other than that which we do? How does it feel to have someone translate us, to relocate us against our wishes, to wake up in a strange bed surrounded by people who don't speak our language and who show no interest in learning it? According to interpretation's many insults, all things are deceivers or dupes, liars or fools. How would you like to be a dream spoken of in the manner recounted above?

Interpretations remove things from their given contexts to ones established by the interpretations, which is why interpretations give us a sense of having our bearings, a sense we do not have when we remain in imagination's uncharted waters. Style understands that one's perceptions of context are part of that context; that if we are perceiving then we are present and so must be included in our accounts. But style avoids attempts to overtly change a given context into one more pleasing and understandable to one's own tastes. For style, the things of the world provide their own contexts and any attempt to alter those contexts for our own ends necessarily affects how we receive and are received by other things. As with the uncertainty principle of physics, our observations cannot help but be part of that which we observe, and so the more overt our self-interest becomes, and the more unrequested guidance we provide through our interpretations, the more we abstract and distort our observations.

Interpretation veneers the grain and knottiness of things. It is a form of explanation, after all, and so it prefers to lay things out flat and seamless, one interpretation smoothly joining the next. How interpretations loves to see its posited meanings flowing uninterrupted one into another. But of course interpretation appropriates only certain characteristics of a thing's presence for use in its interpretations, only appearing to be interested in a thing while it picks its pockets. In the end interpretation is not really interested in things so much as it is interested in its own thoughts about things. Things, including existing interpretations, are just jumping-off points for further interpretations. Interpretations are like people who talk to you at a party while looking over your shoulder for something better to do, a more meaningful conversation, perhaps, or a person more worthy of their time. Sad that such people so rarely seem content to dance with the one that brung 'em.

CHAPTER FOURTEEN

Summaries and Suggestions

We come now to the end of our little book on style. We began by describing the world of style as the things of the world being present before other things. The things of the world are in constant contact and interaction, shaping and reshaping the natures of things as interest and response fill the world with activity. Amidst all of this activity affinities appear, drawing some things into close, intimate relationships with other things. But neither presence, interest, response, nor affinity are creations of the things of the world. Rather they are what give us the apparent world. And the world of appearances is the world of style.

For style, the things of the world are as they appear to be; what you see is what you get. This does not mean, of course, that perception is always up to seeing what it is shown, or that anything is capable of being seen at once in all of its wonder. So style also says that what you get is what you see. One goal of this book has therefore been to encourage more careful and respectful seeing, where seeing is meant as a metaphor for all of our perceiving and imagining abilities.

Style itself has remained undefined throughout our work. Instead we have tried simply to ask what is essential to something appearing as it does? Also left undefined has been the idea of essentials itself. We have suggested, however, that from the perspective of style whatever is present is necessary and whatever is necessary is present. This is in keeping with a recurring theme of this book that we try our best to engage the other things of the world in a manner befitting them. The six essentials of style we have explored, then, are taken as essentials because they help things to appear before the other things of the world.

Aristotle once described soul as an essential, placing it at the center of all things and saying that soul both constitutes a thing while also giving it its particular possibilities of motion. We might similarly imagine our six essentials as all being present in the appearance of each thing, allowing it to appear as it does. Our six essentials are involved with each thing and its actions no matter how small and or seemingly insignificant. A grain of sand is as much a proclamation of style as is a plant or a human and so is worthy of similar interest and respect.

This also suggests that our six essentials are always there in each other, too. A thing's temperament, for example, cannot be separated from the influences of the other five essentials. Nor can we expect our essentials always to be in agreement. I might have the talents needed to be a lawyer, for example, in terms of analytic ability and the like, but not a temperament suited for tedium or a taste suited for tight shoes. Even our affinities need not be shared by all essentials — I might love spending all day in my wood shop but never find the talent for hammer and saw.

We have seen that in some ancient religions the only commandment was to forget no god. Style would similarly have us remember all of the essentials. They are, after all, always there— that is what makes them essential. In the world of style nothing exists in isolation. Indeed for style even isolation is seen as belonging to a tradition proclaimed by its own style.

It is a test of modern imagination whether we can see the things of the world in such a manner. Style is the face of character, but can we any longer read the faces of the world for their character? Can we imagine the rock having talent, the fox living according to taste and tradition, the vine revealed by its tools, the bird learning from its teachers, the sea frothing with temperament? Can we feel the things of the world as purposive and intelligent each in its own way? Can we acknowledge that when we go to market and pick our vegetables for tonight's dinner that we are not the only active participants, that the taste that wants this meal is a gift from elsewhere and that on this day it is the carrots and not the potatoes that want to go home with us? Can we see that our comments about things reveal as much about our need to comment about things as they do about things themselves? Can we see that style touches us before we know we can feel, resonating us with the world's emotions? And can we see that we are always in some imaginative context, always subject to images and influences not of our own making, always tuning in a show already in progress?

For style, this comes down to taking all things as images and in terms of images. The world of style is a field of imagination where things appear and reveal themselves as images to the other things of the world. This harkens to an old view that the goddess of Beauty was necessary in the pantheon of gods not because she was pretty or made things pretty but because she made things appear. It was her role among the other gods to make the things of the world visible and this visibility in turn made possible the opportunities of a sensuous and sensible world. This old idea of beauty as that which appears as itself is in keeping with style, and is the beauty that style proclaims in each thing.

The essentials we have considered are not usually associated with the appearance of things because they have been subsumed by the errors of our age. Through the combined effects of internalization, identity, and interpretation the things of the world have been emptied of their efficacy and significance. And so we habitually talk about having this or that talent or taste, of choosing our traditions and teachers, of creating tools and their use, and of temperament as arising from nature, nurture, or some combination of the two. According to such mistaken formulations all such things ultimately belong to us, can be changed according to our will and whim, and are important primarily for what they say about our inner life and true being.

Style leads us away from the killing fields of such introversions. Style says that we have turned things inside out, rendering things in misshapen forms and then declaring our surprise that the world feels alien and strange. Style offers a way to recover ground lost to such misfortunate habits of the mind.

This is a book about perceiving and appreciating the things of the world and yet it consists almost entirely of ideas and words. This is in keeping with one of the other main themes of this book that ideas and words are themselves proclaimed by style, that they are living images possessed of their own integrity. And so throughout this book we have turned again and again to etymology instead of definition, trying to reclaim the images in our words. Not that our contemporary words are not images in themselves, but under sway of internalization, identity, and interpretation our ability to recognize them as such has faded. By turning to their older, sometimes archaic, meanings we have tried once again to see words as exotic and wonderful. But then this is a book after all, a creation of words and ideas, and so such claims are perhaps to be expected. Like the philosopher who insists on philosophy, it is just like a writer to insist on the beauty and power of words.

We cannot see what we cannot see. The contour of our own face, the gleam in our eyes—such things are visible to the other things of the world but not to us. So, too, are we blind to the attitudes and perspectives, the beliefs and biases, that present us to the other things of the world. Neither my voice on the tape recorder nor the arrogance that others claim to see in my actions sound like me to me. And yet others insist that both are as they appear to be.

Style emphasizes that what is most apparent about us is mostly inaccessible to our so-called personal reflections. Indeed it is precisely where we are the surest, where we are convinced beyond doubt that we speak of the true, the real, and the concrete that we are most blind to the influences that shape us. The ancients did not believe their gods were real any more than we believe that trees are real or the sun is one star among many. Such things are not matters of belief for us; they simply are taken for granted. But taking things for granted reveals our greatest leaps of faith. Who, after all, is the grantor of our certainties? And so the gods are most influential exactly where our pride declares them absent, just as what we declare to be unconscious says nothing about the things of the world and everything about the state of our not knowing. Style reminds us of such limitations and so encourages moderation in our certainties. In fact style introduces us into a world where such claims are unnecessary. It is significant that the cosmology bespoken by style has no need to declare a sunset fact or fiction, a visitor in a dream real or unreal, or love false or true.

Endings encourage summaries and suggestions. At the same time, they let old habits in through the back door. So looking back over our review of the essentials of style and the obstacles that hinder them we might find ourselves asking: Yes, yes I understand how style proclaims all things, but how can a person, me for instance, find and develop his or her style? Given what we have learned about obstacles to style, this response should now be received with recognition and caution. This is a question belonging squarely to the obfuscating traditions of internalization, identity, and interpretation. Asking how to develop my style forgets a basic theme of this book that it is not we who have style but style that has us. Style is already proclaiming us while we struggle to find ourselves elsewhere. Focusing on how to develop my style distracts me from my primary responsibilities to the styles of other things. Ironically, our own styles seem to become the clearer the more we stop looking for them. It is better, then, to focus on the other things of the world and what they have to show us.

If we are curious about our own styles we might instead ask: What do the other things of the world see in me? How do they think I might best serve the talents that they see in me? Over time, what things have turned to me? What have they asked of me? And to what things do I find myself returning? How might I better engage the things to which I am drawn by temperament and taste? How might I do justice to a teacher's example or tradition's memory? And these tools, these wonderful tools, that have collected around me—what do they await, what might we together accomplish?

It is a catastrophic prejudice of the modern mind that such questions are today heard as anthropomorphic projections. For style, such questions can further valuable reflection, but look how different the style of this reflection is from introspective quests for unity or interpretative self-portraiture. Style's reflections constantly lead to the other things of the world and selfless concerns for their welfare. There is nothing secret or repressed in style's considerations because it wants nothing more than to engage the interest and responses of other things. It is not style's style to abstract from things—even the introvert appears as such to the other things of the world, and it is this appearance that is style's abiding concern.

And so style's answer to how to best honor style is to serve well the things of the world. Whatever awareness a thing gains about itself comes ultimately from the presences of the other things of the world, the peculiar interests that motivate and inspire, the responses we give and receive, and the affinities that seek us out as surely as spring refreshes. In an age of internalization, identity, and interpretation where the other things of the world are more and more imagined as fungibles to be managed for maximized benefit to humans (save the wilderness for our children, and so on) style encourages a counter-cultural move based on humility and respect. Style reminds us that internalization has not shown itself prone to saving things but to destroying them. If the wilderness needs saving, it is because internalization has put it at risk by overstepping natural boundaries. We owe such restitution to the wilderness on its own behalf, not to satisfy human posterity. The mountains are not beautiful because we say they are beautiful.

Style, then, casts a rather unblinking eye. Morality is given by the context of the things perceived instead of moralisms imposed, so style need not blush or shield its eyes. The horrors that sometimes go along with things cannot be vanquished by utopian thoughts that lead us to nowhere, so style need not turn away from what is before it. Privacy is itself a thing to be appreciated, so style need not peek behind drawn curtains. What is there is enough for style. It sounds so simple-minded. And yet through style we find that the complexities of things encourage us to complexities in kind. So much wonder.

We learn about style from the other things of the world. There is nowhere else to go so far as style is concerned. Our thoughts about ourselves are of course things in their own right, but they, too, are proclamations by style. They can be appreciated for what they are, reflected on in terms of their essentials. What admixture of humours speaks in such a fashion? What tools do our thoughts about ourselves carry in their pockets? What marks do they leave on the other things of the world? And so on. But in the world of style our thoughts about ourselves are part of the body politic that comprises the many things of the world. Ours is but one voice among others, worthy of the respect it is due, yes, but no more.

Style encourages proper etiquette toward the things of the world. If, as we have contended, we are dependent in the most basic ways imaginable on the other things of the world, and if the other things of the world are similarly dependent upon us, then what could be more necessary than imagining our fellows with a charity and discipline based on honest experience? If the modern mind feels such etiquette as being outmoded and stiff, this is largely because the modern mind has become callused by its own rudeness.

A mind under sway of the obstacles we have reviewed can be a boorish thing. It often seems incapable of going with any flow other than its own stream of consciousness or of setting aside its own habits to learn from the things of the world how they do things. Style tries to educate the mind about such shortcomings and asks that we approach the other things of the world with good manners and clean hands.

If style would educate us through its proclamations we might educate style by attending to the work is sets before us. Nothing in this book should be taken as supporting a mindless wallowing in one's own nature. First because this book rejects the idea of "one's own nature." And second because style is not something that is "known" to us but rather is apparent to the other things of the world. Style calls for the careful and prolonged study of things as they are given to us by their styles.

The old alchemists had a strange saying that their work was an *opus contra naturam*, a work against nature. It is difficult to know what they meant by this, but if we take nature in its internalized, identified, and interpreted form then we could likewise say that style is a work against nature, a work against the processes that would reduce the things of the world to their meaning and significance for the human individual. Style keeps us in a world of wonder and mystery, tempering our experience and knowledge with humility and restraint. Style requires great discipline and a well-educated sense of propriety and respect. And so this book has tried to help us look differently at that hammer in our hand, seeing it not as a product of our own invention but as a presence of authority and learning that offers its own opportunities to a waiting world.

The zoologist Adolf Portmann was a champion of the world of appearances, constantly calling attention to the beauty and significance of plant and animal life in its many forms. As a scientist he worked hard to overcome the dualistic tendencies of his tradition, especially the inner/outer legacy of Descartes. Portmann urged fresh thinking here, asking that we once again see that there is no clear line between what is apparent and what is not. He offers a nice summary for many of the ideas we have discussed:

> We should not deprecate what appears on [the] surface by thinking of it as a 'front,' an incidental extra which is plastered over a far more genuine and authentic 'inside.' No greater allotment of reality or honor can be ascribed to what is

hidden than to this appearance we derive from an opaque, patterned and designed outermost surface. Indeed the inwardness of the living thing is a non-dimensional reality which is spatially located neither in a spatial inside nor in a center. Rather, an active 'medium' or 'midst' is present within the entire animal. The potencies implicit in fragrances or sound-production also belong to the sensible realities of the realm of appearances: that realm is always active in its casting itself abroad into the world, and, in so doing, it acts on a sensitive inwardness which experiences that activity. Whether through sight, smell, or sound, appearance is always working on the surroundings and thereby also on an inwardness which assimilates these effects and which itself experiences appearance. This activity which affects the sense extends the reach of the individual and adds to its experience. However, such an enrichment of the animal's communal life should not be seized upon as the origin of social forms of life. For, that enrichment does not locate the origin of social forms of life in the primary stage where we find isolated individuals. Rather this enrichment acts on an already prepared foundation of 'sympathy' or affinity through the structures by which the animals make themselves known. It is only this pre-disposition which, transcending the solitary mode of life from the very beginning, leads to the recognition and the search for others of like kind; and, in fact it is just this very disposition which makes it possible for the unfolding of that system of self identification to others. The individual is never alone, but, through its dispositions, it is already more than a solitary individual. (*Essays in Philosophical Zoology*, pp. 25-26.)

Style extends such extraordinary ideas to the styles of all things. You can see how difficult is has become to talk about things without falling into old traps. How difficult it is for a scientist to talk of "non-dimensional realities," or to recognize that all things come into being already belonging to a welcoming world. And yet we find echoes of Portmann's words in many of the themes of this book—the attempt to avoid dualism, the refusal to denigrate appearance for the sake of inner truth, the constant "casting abroad" of the many things of the world, the basic importance of affinity, and the essential multiplicity of all things. It is as if, when we turn our attentions to matters of style, we end up speaking in a manner that style prefers.

Where Portmann asked his colleagues to expand their imaginations about plant and animal life, this book asks that we similarly extend our imagination to make room for all of the things of the world. Style takes things as they come and is content with things as they are even though it loves to work with things, adorning and arranging for better effect. Style is under no pressure to extract meaning or spin interpretations, it does not quest for identity or definition, or claim that the life we feel in the other things of the world is a projection from within our own minds. Having said this, style is aware that it, too, is a limited perspective. Even as style appreciates a painting or a sunset it is aware that others will see these things differently and that these perspectives offer important angles worth appreciating in their own right. For style there is room for everything. Style objects only when other perspectives claim superior or exclusive status and thereby curtail further imagining.

In closing, a final mystery also brought to our attention by Portmann. Not until modern times has it become possible for humans to explore the deepest waters of the oceans. These are regions of perpetual night and encompassing darkness. Animals there have no eyes. And yet when the tiny submarines that plow these depths turn their spotlights on this inky world they find there animals of extraordinary beauty and design. Here is a purple octopus and there a feathered red anemone. A crystalline shrimp swims by. How can this be? Why are these things not bland and pale as might befit a world without light or eyes? We have said that style is the presence of things before other things and yet here are sights for which there seems to be no seer.

Portmann referred to such qualities in things as "unaddressed phenomena," and raised the possibility that things do not display for the purpose of being seen by others but because perhaps display is so basic that it does not need to be perceived by others. If so, then style as described in this book, with all of its interest and fascination with the appearance of things, is hardly a final word. Maybe style proclaims the things of the world simply because that is what style enjoys doing. Maybe style is not dependent upon appearances but gives rise to the very possibility of appearances. And maybe the sheer beauty of things is a bonus, a gift that, once unwrapped of our assumptions, reveals a cosmos adorned beyond imagining.

Writings that Helped

Ashton, Dore, ed. *Twentieth-Century Artists on Art*. New York: Pantheon Books, 1985.

Barfield, Owen. *History in English Words*. Great Barrington, MA: Lindisfarne Press, 1988.

Berry, Patricia. *Echo's Subtle Body*. Dallas: Spring Publications, 1982.

Edward, Paul, ed. *The Encyclopedia of Philosophy*. 8 vols. New York: MacMillan, 1972.

Flexner, Stuart, ed. *The Random House Dictionary of the English Language*. 2nd ed. New York: Random House, 1987.

Freeberg, David. *The Power of Images*. Chicago, IL: University of Chicago Press, 1991.

Freud, Sigmund. *The Interpretation of Dreams*. Trans. James Strachey. New York: Avon Books, 1965.

Goldwater, Robert and Marco Treves, eds. *Artists on Art from the 14th to the 20th Century*. New York: Pantheon Books, 1972.

Goertzel, Victor and Mildred Goertzel. *Cradles of Eminence*. Boston, MA: Little, Brown & Company, 1962.

[The works of James Hillman, especially:]

Hillman, James. *Re-Visioning Psychology*. New York: Harper and Row, 1975.

_____. *The Force of Character and the Lasting Life*. New York: Random House, 1999.

_____. *The Soul's Code*. New York: Random House, 1996.

_____ and Margot McLean. *Dream Animals*. San Francisco, CA: Chronicle Books, 1997.

Johnson, Paul. *The Renaissance*. New York: Modern Library, 2000.

Klibansky, Raymond, Erwin Panofsky, and Fritz Saxl. *Saturn and Melancholy*. New York: Basic Books, 1964.

[The works of Thomas Moore, especially:]

Moore, Thomas. *Care of the Soul*. New York: HarperCollins, 1992.

_____. *Dark Eros*. Dallas, TX: Spring Publications, 1990.

_____. *The Planets Within*. Great Barrington, MA: Lindisfarne Press, 1990.

Onians, C. T., ed. *The Oxford Dictionary of English Etymology*. Oxford, UK: Oxford University Press, 1985.

[The works of Walker Percy, especially:]

Percy, Walter. *Diagnosing the Modern Malaise*. New Orleans, LA: Faust Publishing, 1985.

_____. *Lost in the Cosmos*. New York: Farrar, Strauss & Giroux, 1983.

_____. *Love in the Ruins*. New York: Farrar, Strauss & Giroux, 1971.

_____. *The State of the Novel*. New Orleans, LA: Faust Publishing, 1987.

Portmann, Adolf. *Animal Forms and Patterns*. Trans. Hella Czech. London: Faber and Faber, 1961.

_____. *Essays in Philosophical Zoology*. Trans. Richard Carter. Lampeter, Wales: The Edwin Mellen Press, 1990.

_____. "The Orientation and World-Relation of Animals." Trans. Richard Carter. *Spring 1986*.

_____. "What Living Form Means to Us." Trans. Richard Carter. *Spring 1982*.

Rilke, Rainer Maria. *Letters to a Young Poet*. Trans. M. D. Herter Norton. New York: W. W. Norton, 1962.

Sells, Benjamin. "An Eye Grafted on the Heart." *Eranos Yearbook 1999*. Woodstock, CT: Spring Journal, 1999.

_____. "Fundamentalism as a Variety of Rational Experience." *Spring 2001*.

_____, ed. *Working with Images: The Theoretical Base of Archetypal Psychology*. Woodstock, CT: Spring Publications, 2000.

Skeat, Walter. *A Concise Etymological Dictionary of the English Language*. New York: Perigee Books, 1980.

Spring Journal, issues 1970 to present, published in various locations, currently in New Orleans, Louisiana.

Tocqueville, Alexis. *Democracy in America*. Ed. Phillips Bradley. Trans. Henry Reeve. 2 vols. New York: Vintage Classics, 1990.

Vasari, Giorgio. *The Lives of the Artists*. Trans. Julia and Peter Bondanella. Oxford, UK: Oxford University Press, 1991.

Watkins, Mary. *Waking Dreams*. Dallas, TX: Spring Publications, 1984.

Willey, Basil. *The Eighteenth Century Background: Studies on the Idea of Nature in the Thought of the Period*. Boston, MA: Beacon Press, 1964.

_____. *The Seventeenth Century Background: Studies in the Thought of the Age in Relation to Poetry and Religion.* New York: Columbia University Press, 1958.

Wilson, Frank. *The Hand.* New York: Vintage Books, 1999.

Wittkower, Rudolf and Margot Wittkower. *Born Under Saturn.* New York: Norton, 1963.

Other Things that Helped

I would like to thank the following for their influences on this book:

My teachers, especially James Hillman, Benjamin Ladner, and Thomas Moore;

My family, and especially my late brother, David H. Sells, Jr., who was always there to protect and champion what he saw in me;

My wife and step-daughter, Tori and Sophie, who bring style to life and life to style;

A special thank you to Jay Livernois;

My colleagues, especially Peter Acheson, Stephen Aizenstat, David Barton, Patricia Berry, Richard Carter, Margot McLean, Rudolf Ritsema, Christa Robinson, Shantena Sabbadini, Gary Shunk, Dennis Slattery, Joanne Stroud, Gail Thomas, and Megan Wells;

The organizations and publications that allowed me to present and refine many of the ideas in this book, especially the Eranos Foundation, Pacifica Graduate Institute, the Dallas Institute for Humanities and Culture, Green Street, the Institute for the Study of Imagination, *Spring Journal*, and *Salt Journal*;

Chicago, the Outer Banks of North Carolina, and the waters that make them;

The Dragon Fleet and its uncompromising pleasures;

Nancy Cater, Greg Mogenson, and Michael Mendis of Spring Journal Books for their insight and dedication to the art of book-making;

And the many presences unrecognized by me who took an interest in this book and moved things along when times were right.

SPRING JOURNAL BOOKS

The book publishing imprint of *Spring Journal,*
the oldest Jungian psychology journal in the world

STUDIES IN ARCHETYPAL PSYCHOLOGY SERIES
Series Editor: Greg Mogenson

Collected English Papers, Wolfgang Giegerich
  Vol. 1: *The Neurosis of Psychology: Primary Papers Towards a Critical Psychology,* ISBN 1-882670-42-6, 284 pp., $20.00
  Vol. 2: *Technology and the Soul,* ISBN 1-882670-43-4
  Vol. 3: *Soul-Violence* ISBN 1-882670-44-2
  Vol. 4: *The Soul Always Thinks* ISBN 1-882670-45-0

Dialectics & Analytical Psychology: The El Capitan Canyon Seminar, Wolfgang Giegerich, David L. Miller, and Greg Mogenson, ISBN 1-882670-92-2, 136 pp., $20.00

Northern Gnosis: Thor, Baldr, and the Volsungs in the Thought of Freud and Jung, Greg Mogenson, ISBN 1-882670-90-6, 140 pp., $20.00

Raids on the Unthinkable: Freudian and Jungian Psychoanalyses, Paul Kugler, ISBN 1-882670-91-4, 160 pp., $20.00

The Wounded Researcher: A Depth Psychological Approach to Research, Robert Romanyshyn, ISBN 1-882670-47-7

The Sunken Quest, the Wasted Fisher, the Pregnant Fish: Postmodern Reflections on Depth Psychology, Ronald Schenk, ISBN: 1-882670-48-5, $20.00

Fire in the Stone: The Alchemy of Desire, Stanton Marlan, ed., ISBN 1-882670-49-3, 206 pp., $22.95

HONORING DAVID L. MILLER

Disturbances in the Field: Essays in Honor of David L. Miller, Christine Downing, ed., ISBN 1-882670-37-X, 318 pp., $23.95

THE DAVID L. MILLER TRILOGY

Three Faces of God: Traces of the Trinity in Literature and Life, David L. Miller, ISBN 1-882670-94-9, 197 pp., $20.00

Christs: Meditations on Archetypal Images in Christian Theology, David L. Miller, ISBN 1-882670-93-0, 249 pp., $20.00

Hells and Holy Ghosts: A Theopoetics of Christian Belief, David L. Miller, ISBN 1-882670-99-3, 238 pp., $20.00

THE ELECTRA SERIES

Electra: Tracing a Feminine Myth through the Western Imagination, Nancy Cater, ISBN 1-882670-98-1, 137 pp., $20.00

Fathers' Daughters: Breaking the Ties That Bind, Maureen Murdock, ISBN 1-882670-31-0, 258 pp., $20.00

Daughters of Saturn: From Father's Daughter to Creative Woman, Patricia Reis, ISBN 1-882670-32-9, 361 pp., $23.95

Women's Mysteries: Twoard a Poetics of Gender, Christine Downing, ISBN 1-882670-99-XX, 237 pp., $20.00

Gods in Our Midst: Mythological Images of the Masculine—A Woman's View, Christine Downing, ISBN 1-882670-28-0, 152 pp., $20.00

Journey through Menopause: A Personal Rite of Passage, Christine Downing, ISBN 1-882670-33-7, 172 pp., $20.00

Portrait of the Blue Lady: The Character of Melancholy, Lyn Cowan, ISBN 1-882670-96-5, 314 pp., $23.95

MORE SPRING JOURNAL BOOKS

Field, Form, and Fate: Patterns in Mind, Nature, and Psyche, Michael Conforti, ISBN 1-882670-40-X, 181 pp., $20.00

Dark Voices: The Genesis of Roy Hart Theatre, Noah Pikes, ISBN 1-882670-19-1, 155 pp., $20.00

The World Turned Inside Out: Henry Corbin and Islamic Mysticism, Tom Cheetham, ISBN 1-882670-24-8, 210 pp., $20.00

Teachers of Myth: Interviews on Educational and Psychological Uses of Myth with Adolescents, Maren Tonder Hansen, ISBN 1-882670-89-2, 73 pp., $15.95

Following the Reindeer Woman: Path of Peace and Harmony, Linda Schierse Leonard, ISBN 1-882670-95-7, 229 pp., $20.00

An Oedipus—The Untold Story: A Ghostly Mythodrama in One Act, Armando Nascimento Rosa, ISBN 1-882670-38-8, 103 pp., $20.00

Psyche and the Sacred: Spirituality Beyond Religion, Lionel Corbett, ISBN 1-882670-34-5, $23.95.

The Dreaming Way: Dreamwork and Art for Remembering and Recovery, Patricia Reis and Susan Snow, ISBN 1-882670-46-9, $24.95

Living with Jung: "Enterviews" with Jungian Analysts, Volume I, Robert and Janis Henderson, ISBN 1-882670-35-3, 249 pp., $21.95.

Terraspychology: Re-engaging the Soul of Place, Craig Chalquist, ISBN1-882670-65-5, 162 pp., $20.00.

HOW TO ORDER:

Write to us at: Spring Journal Books, 627 Ursulines Street # 7, New Orleans, Louisiana 70116, USA

Call us at: (504) 524-5117

Fax us at: (504) 558-0088

Visit our website at: www.springjournalandbooks.com